Big Data Visualization

Learn effective tools and techniques to separate big data into manageable and logical components for efficient data visualization

James D. Miller

BIRMINGHAM - MUMBAI

Big Data Visualization

First published: February 2017

Production reference: 1230217

Published by Packt Publishing Ltd.
Livery Place
35 Livery Street
Birmingham
B3 2PB, UK.
ISBN 978-1-78528-194-5

www.packtpub.com

Credits

Author

James D. Miller

Reviewers

Dave Wentzel

Commissioning Editor

Veena Pagare

Acquisition Editor

Tushar Gupta

Content Development Editor

Sumeet Sawant

Technical Editor

Sneha Hanchate

Copy Editor

Laxmi Subramanian

Project Coordinator

Shweta H Birwatkar

Proofreader

Safis Editing

Indexer

Aishwarya Gangawane

Graphics

Tania Dutta

Production Coordinator

Arvindkumar Gupta

About the Author

James D. Miller is an IBM certified expert, creative innovator, and accomplished Director, Sr. Project Leader, and Application/System Architect with more than 35 years of extensive applications, system design, and development experience across multiple platforms and technologies.

His experiences and specialties include introducing customers to new and sometimes disruptive technologies and platforms, integrating with IBM Watson Analytics, cloud migrations, Cognos BI, TM1 and web architecture design, systems analysis, GUI design and testing, data and database modeling and systems analysis, design, and the development of OLAP, Client/Server, Web and Mainframe applications and systems utilizing IBM Watson Analytics, IBM Cognos BI and TM1 (TM1 rules, TI, TM1Web and Planning Manager), Cognos Framework Manager, dynaSight/ArcPlan, ASP, DHTML, XML, IIS, MS Visual Basic and VBA, Visual Studio, Perl, Splunk, WebSuite, MS SQL server, ORACLE, SYBASE Server, and more.

His responsibilities have also included all aspects of Windows and SQL solution development and design, including analysis; GUI (and Web site) design; data modeling; table, screen/form and script development; SQL (and remote stored procedures and triggers) development/testing; test preparation; and the management and training of programming staff. His other experience includes the development of ETL infrastructure such as data transfer automation between mainframe (DB2, Lawson, Great Plains, and so on) systems and client/server SQL server and web-based applications and integration of enterprise applications and data sources.

Mr. James D. Miller has acted as an Internet Applications Development manager responsible for the design, development, QA, and delivery of multiple websites, including online trading applications, warehouse process control, scheduling systems, and administrative and control applications. He was also responsible for the design, development, and administration of a web-based financial reporting system for a 450-million-dollar organization, reporting directly to the CFO and his executive team.

Mr. Miller has also been responsible for managing and directing multiple resources in various management roles, including project and team leader, lead developer, and applications development director.

Mr. Miller has authored Cognos TM1 Developers Certification Guide, Mastering Splunk, Learning IBM Watson Analytics, and a number of whitepapers on best practices such as Establishing a Center of Excellence, and continues to post blogs on a number of relevant topics based upon personal experiences and industry best practices. Jim is a perpetual learner who continues to pursue experiences and certifications, and currently holds the following current technical certifications:

- IBM Certified Business Analyst - Cognos TM1
- IBM Cognos TM1 Master 385 Certification (perfect score of 100% on exam)
- IBM Certified Advanced Solution Expert - Cognos TM1
- IBM Cognos TM1 10.1 Administrator Certification C2020-703 (perfect score of 100% on exam)
- IBM OpenPages Developer Fundamentals C2020-001-ENU (98% on exam)
- IBM Cognos 10 BI Administrator C2020-622 (98% on exam)
- IBM Cognos 10 BI Professional C2020-180

His specialties include the evaluation and introduction of innovative and disruptive technologies, cloud migration, big data, IBM Watson Analytics, Cognos BI and TM1 application Design and Development, OLAP, Visual Basic, SQL Server, Forecasting and Planning, International Application Development, Business Intelligence, Project Development and Delivery, and process improvement.

About the Reviewer

Dave Wentzel is a Data Solutions Architect for Microsoft. He helps customers with their Azure Digital Transformation focused on data science, big data, and SQL Server. After working with customers, he provides feedback and learnings to the product groups at Microsoft to make better solutions. Dave has been working with SQL Server for many years, and with MDX and SSAS since they were in their infancy. Dave shares his experiences at `http://davewentzel.com`. He's always looking for new customers. Would you like to engage?

www.PacktPub.com

For support files and downloads related to your book, please visit www.PacktPub.com.

Did you know that Packt offers eBook versions of every book published, with PDF and ePub files available? You can upgrade to the eBook version at www.PacktPub.com and as a print book customer, you are entitled to a discount on the eBook copy. Get in touch with us at service@packtpub.com for more details.

At www.PacktPub.com, you can also read a collection of free technical articles, sign up for a range of free newsletters and receive exclusive discounts and offers on Packt books and eBooks.

https://www.packtpub.com/mapt

Get the most in-demand software skills with Mapt. Mapt gives you full access to all Packt books and video courses, as well as industry-leading tools to help you plan your personal development and advance your career.

Why subscribe?

- Fully searchable across every book published by Packt
- Copy and paste, print, and bookmark content
- On demand and accessible via a web browser

Customer Feedback

Thank you for purchasing this Packt book. We take our commitment to improving our content and products to meet your needs seriously—that's why your feedback is so valuable. Whatever your feelings about your purchase, please consider leaving a review on this book's Amazon page. Not only will this help us, more importantly, it will also help others in the community to make an informed decision about the resources that they invest in to learn.

You can also review for us on a regular basis by joining our reviewers' club. **If you're interested in joining, or would like to learn more about the benefits we offer, please contact us**: customerreviews@packtpub.com.

Table of Contents

Preface

The concepts and models necessary to efficiently and effectively visualize big data can be daunting but are not unobtainable. Unfortunately, when it comes to big data, many of the available data visualization tools, with their rudimentary functions and features, are somewhat ineffective.

Using basic analytical concepts (reviewed in this book), you'll learn to use some of the most popular open source tools (and others) to meet these challenges and approach the task of big data visualization to support better decision making.

What this book covers

Chapter 1, *Introduction to Big Data Visualization,* – starts out by providing a simple explanation of just what data visualization is and then provides a quick overview of various generally accepted data visualization concepts.

Chapter 2, *Access, Speed, and Storage with Hadoop,* aims to target the challenge of storing and accessing large volumes and varieties (structured or unstructured) of data offering working examples demonstrating solutions for effectively addressing these issues.

Chapter 3, *Understanding Your Data Using R,* explores the idea of adding context to the big data you are working on with R.

Chapter 4, *Addressing Big Data Quality,* talks about categorized data quality and the challenges big data brings to them. In addition, examples demonstrating concepts for effectively addressing these areas are covered.

Chapter 5, *Displaying Results Using D3,* explores the process of visualizing data using a web browser and Data-Driven Documents (D3) to present results from your big data analysis projects.

Chapter 6, *Dashboards for Big Data - Tableau,* introduces Tableau as a data visualization tool that can be used to construct dashboards and provides working examples demonstrating solutions for effectively presenting results from your big data analysis in a real-time dashboard format.

Chapter 7, *Dealing with Outliers Using Python*, focuses on the topic of dealing with outliers and other anomalies as they relate to big data visualization, and introduces the Python language with working examples of effectively dealing with data.

Chapter 8, *Big Data Operational Intelligence with Splunk*, offers working examples demonstrating solutions for valuing big data by gaining operational intelligence (using Splunk).

What you need for this book

Most of the tools and technologies used in this book are open source and available for no charge. All of the others offer free trials for evaluation. With this book, and some basic exposure to data analysis (or basic programming concepts) the reader will be able to gain valuable insights to the world of big data visualization!

Who this book is for

The target audience of this book are data analysts and those with at least a basic knowledge of big data analysis who now want to learn interesting approaches to big data visualization in order to make their analysis more valuable. Readers who possess adequate knowledge of big data platform tools such as Hadoop or have exposure to programming languages such as R can use this book to learn additional approaches (using various technologies) for addressing the inherent challenges of visualizing big data.

Conventions

In this book, you will find a number of text styles that distinguish between different kinds of information. Here are some examples of these styles and an explanation of their meaning.

Code words in text, database table names, folder names, filenames, file extensions, pathnames, dummy URLs, user input, and Twitter handles are shown as follows: "The next lines of code reads the link and assigns it to the to the `BeautifulSoup` function."

A block of code is set as follows:

```
for row in reader:
        if (row['Denomination']) == 'Penny':
          if int(row['Coin-in'])<2000:
             x += int(row['Coin-in'])
          row_count += 1
```

When we wish to draw your attention to a particular part of a code block, the relevant lines or items are set in bold:

```
row_count = 0
    aver_coin_in = 0.0
    x = 0.0
    y = 999
    z = 0.0
```

New terms and **important words** are shown in bold. Words that you see on the screen, for example, in menus or dialog boxes, appear in the text like this: "In order to download new modules, we will go to **Files | Settings | Project Name | Project Interpreter**."

 Warnings or important notes appear in a box like this.

 Tips and tricks appear like this.

Reader feedback

Feedback from our readers is always welcome. Let us know what you think about this book-what you liked or disliked. Reader feedback is important for us as it helps us develop titles that you will really get the most out of. To send us general feedback, simply e-mail feedback@packtpub.com, and mention the book's title in the subject of your message. If there is a topic that you have expertise in and you are interested in either writing or contributing to a book, see our author guide at www.packtpub.com/authors.

Customer support

Now that you are the proud owner of a Packt book, we have a number of things to help you to get the most from your purchase.

Downloading the example code

You can download the example code files for this book from your account at `http://www.packtpub.com`. If you purchased this book elsewhere, you can visit `http://www.packtpub.com/support` and register to have the files e-mailed directly to you.

You can download the code files by following these steps:

1. Log in or register to our website using your e-mail address and password.
2. Hover the mouse pointer on the **SUPPORT** tab at the top.
3. Click on **Code Downloads & Errata**.
4. Enter the name of the book in the **Search** box.
5. Select the book for which you're looking to download the code files.
6. Choose from the drop-down menu where you purchased this book from.
7. Click on **Code Download**.

Once the file is downloaded, please make sure that you unzip or extract the folder using the latest version of:

- WinRAR / 7-Zip for Windows
- Zipeg / iZip / UnRarX for Mac
- 7-Zip / PeaZip for Linux

The code bundle for the book is also hosted on GitHub at `https://github.com/PacktPublishing/Big-Data-Visualization`. We also have other code bundles from our rich catalog of books and videos available at `https://github.com/PacktPublishing/`. Check them out!

Downloading the color images of this book

We also provide you with a PDF file that has color images of the screenshots/diagrams used in this book. The color images will help you better understand the changes in the output. You can download this file from `https://www.packtpub.com/sites/default/files/downloads/BigDataVisualization_ColorImages.pdf`.

Errata

Although we have taken every care to ensure the accuracy of our content, mistakes do happen. If you find a mistake in one of our books-maybe a mistake in the text or the code-we would be grateful if you could report this to us. By doing so, you can save other readers from frustration and help us improve subsequent versions of this book. If you find any errata, please report them by visiting http://www.packtpub.com/submit-errata, selecting your book, clicking on the **Errata Submission Form** link, and entering the details of your errata. Once your errata are verified, your submission will be accepted and the errata will be uploaded to our website or added to any list of existing errata under the Errata section of that title.

To view the previously submitted errata, go to https://www.packtpub.com/books/content/supportand enter the name of the book in the search field. The required information will appear under the **Errata** section.

Piracy

Piracy of copyrighted material on the Internet is an ongoing problem across all media. At Packt, we take the protection of our copyright and licenses very seriously. If you come across any illegal copies of our works in any form on the Internet, please provide us with the location address or website name immediately so that we can pursue a remedy.

Please contact us at copyright@packtpub.com with a link to the suspected pirated material.

We appreciate your help in protecting our authors and our ability to bring you valuable content.

Questions

If you have a problem with any aspect of this book, you can contact us at questions@packtpub.com, and we will do our best to address the problem.

1
Introduction to Big Data Visualization

Since this is the first chapter, it may be considered prudent to start out by providing a simple explanation of just what data visualization is and then a quick overview of various generally accepted data visualization concepts.

From there, we will proceed by pointing out the specific challenges that big data brings–to the practice of visualizing data–and then finally we will tee up a number of approaches for successfully creating valuable visualizations using big data sources.

After completing this chapter, the reader will be ready to start with the practical big data visualization examples covered in this book's subsequent chapters; each of which will focus on a specific big data visualization topic, using a specific trending tool or technology thought to be well fitted (note that other tools or technologies may be available) to address that particular topic or challenge.

We'll break down this first chapter into:

- An explanation of data visualization
- Conventional data visualization concepts
- Challenges of big data visualization
- Approaches to big data visualization

An explanation of data visualization

So what is data visualization? Simply put, one can think of the two words, data meaning information/numbers and visualization meaning picturing, or picturing the information as shown in the following figure:

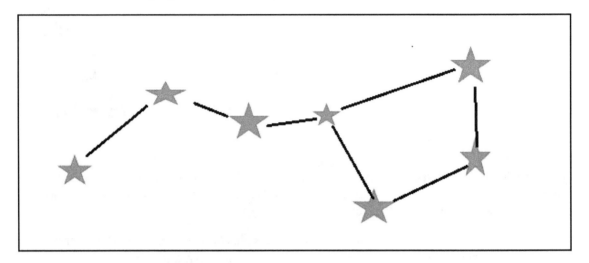

Perhaps a simplistic example that can be used to define data visualization is the practice of striking lines between stars in the night sky to create an image.

Imagine certain stars as the data points you are interested in (among the billions of other stars that are visible in the sky) and connecting them in a certain order to create a picture to help one visualize the constellation.

Voila! Data visualization!

Nowadays, it is reported within the industry that data visualization is regarded by many disciplines as the modern equivalent of visual communication.

Okay, so then what is the point of or chief objective of visual communication or visualizing your data?

The main point (although there are other goals and objectives) when leveraging data visualization is to make something complex appear simple (or in our star example earlier, perhaps to make a data pattern more visible to a somewhat untrained eye).

Communicating a particular point or simplifying the complexities of mountains of data does not require the use of data visualization, but in some way today's world might demand it. That is, the majority of the readers of this book would most likely agree that scanning numerous worksheets, spreadsheets, or reports is mundane and tedious at best, while looking at charts and graphs is typically much easier on the eyes. Additionally, the fact is that we humans are able to process even very large amounts of data much quicker when the data is presented graphically. Therefore, data visualization is a way to convey concepts in a universal manner, allowing your audience or target to quickly get your point.

Other motives for using data visualization include:

- To explain the data or put the data in context (that is, highlight demographical statistics)
- To solve a specific problem, (for example, identifying problem areas within a particular business model)
- To explore the data to reach a better understanding or add clarity (that is, what periods of time does this data span?)
- To highlight or illustrate otherwise invisible data (such as isolating outliers residing in the data)
- To predict, for example, potential sales volumes (perhaps based upon seasonality sales statistics)

With computers, technology, and the corporate business landscape changing so rapidly today (and all indications are that it will continue to change at an even faster pace in the future), what can be considered the future of the art of data visualization?

As per *Data Visualization: The future of data visualization*, Towler, 2015:

> *"Data visualization is entering a new era. Emerging sources of intelligence, theoretical developments, and advances in multidimensional imaging are reshaping the potential value that analytics and insights can provide, with visualization playing a key role."*

With big data getting bigger (and bigger!), it is safe to undertake the notion that the use of data visualization will only continue to grow, to evolve, and to be of outstanding value. In addition, how one approaches the process and practice of data visualization will need to grow and evolve as well.

Conventional data visualization concepts

Let's start out this section by clarifying what we mean when we say conventional.

In the context of this book, when I say conventional, I am referring to the ideas and methods that have been used with some level of success within the industry over time (for data visualization).

Although it seems that every day, new technologies and practices are being discovered, developed, and deployed providing new and different options for performing ever more ingenious real-time (or near real time) data visualization, understanding the basic concepts for visualizing data is still essential.

To that point, gaining an understanding of just how to go about choosing the correct or most effective visualization method is essential.

To make that choice, one typically needs to establish:

- The size and volume of the data to be visualized.
- The data's cardinality and context.
- What is it you are trying to communicate? What is the point that you want to communicate?
- Who is your audience? Who will consume this information?
- What kind or type of visual might best convey your message to your audience?

 We have also been realistic that sometimes the approach taken or method used is solely based upon your time and budget.

Based on the earlier and perhaps other particulars–and you most likely are already familiar with these–the most common visualization methods/types include:

- Table
- Histogram
- Scatter plot
- Line, bar, pie, area, flow, and bubble charts
- Data series or a combination of charts
- Time line
- Venn diagrams, data flow diagrams, and **entity relationship** (**ER**) diagrams

As I've mentioned earlier, as and when needs arise, newer or lesser known options are becoming more main stream.

These include the following:

- Word/Text/Tag clouds
- Network diagrams
- Parallel coordinates
- Tree mapping
- Cone trees
- Semantic networks

Each of the earlier mentioned data visualization types/methods speak to a particular scenario or target audience better than others–it all depends. Learning to make the appropriate choice comes from experience as well as (sometimes) a bit of trial and error.

Training options

Due to the popularity of data visualization, there exist many formal training options, (classroom and online) and new and unique training curriculums are becoming available every day.

Coursework includes topics such as:

- Channeling an audience
- Understanding data
- Determining informational hierarchies
- Sketching and wire framing
- Defining a narrative

Challenges of big data visualization

We're assuming that you have some background with the topic of data visualization and therefore the earlier deliberations were just enough to refresh your memory and sharpen your appetite for the real purpose of this book.

Big data

Let's take a pause here to define big data.

A large assemblage of data and datasets that are so large or complex that traditional data processing applications are inadequate and data about every aspect of our lives has all been used to define or refer to big data.

In 2001, then Gartner analyst Doug Laney introduced the 3Vs concept (refer to the following link `http://blogs.gartner.com/doug-laney/files/2012/01/ad949-3D-Data-Management-Controlling-Data-Volume-Velocity-and-Variety.pdf`). The 3Vs, according to Doug Laney, are volume, variety, and velocity. The 3Vs make up the dimensionality of big data: volume (or the measurable amount of data), variety (meaning the number of types of data), and velocity (referring to the speed of processing or dealing with that data).

With this concept in mind, all aspects of big data become increasingly challenging and as these dimensions increase or expand they will also encumber the ability to effectively visualize the data.

Using Excel to gauge your data

Look at the following figure and remember that Excel is not a tool to determine whether your data qualifies as big data:

If your data is too big for Microsoft Excel, it still really doesn't necessarily qualify as big data. In fact, gigabytes of data still are manageable with various techniques, enterprise, and even open source tools, especially with the lower cost of storage today. It is important to be able to realistically size the data that you will be using in an analytic or visualization project before selecting an approach or technology (keeping in mind expected data growth rates).

Pushing big data higher

As the following figure illustrates, the aforementioned **Volume**, **Variety**, and **Velocity** have and will continue to lift **Big Data** into the future:

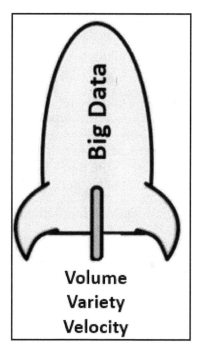

The 3Vs

Let's take a moment to further examine the Vs.

Volume

Volume involves determining or calculating how much of something there is, or in the case of big data, how much of something there will be. Here is a thought provoking example:

How fast does moon dust pile up?

As written by Megan Gannon in 2014, (http://www.space.com/23694-moon-dust-mystery-apollo-data.html), a revisited trove of data from NASA's Apollo missions more than 40 years ago is helping scientists answer a lingering lunar question: how fast does moon dust build up? The answer: it would take 1,000 years for a layer of moon dust about a millimeter (0.04 inches) thick to accumulate (big data accumulates much quicker than moon dust!).

With every click of a mouse, big data grows to be petabytes (1,024 terabytes) or even Exabyte's (1,024 petabytes) consisting of billions to trillions of records generated from millions of people and machines.

Although it's been reported (for example, you can refer to the following link: http://blog.sqlauthority.com/2013/07/21/sql-server-what-is-the-maximum-relation al-database-size-supported-by-single-instance/) that structured or relational database technology could support applications capable of scaling up to 1 petabyte of storage, it doesn't take a lot of thought to understand with that kind of volume it won't be easy to handle capably, and the accumulation rate of big data isn't slowing any time soon.

It's the case of big, bigger (and we haven't even approached determining), and biggest yet!

Velocity

Velocity is the rate or pace at which something is occurring. The measured velocity experience can and usually does change over time. Velocities directly affect outcomes.

Previously, we lived and worked in a batch environment, meaning we formulate a question (perhaps what is our most popular product?), submit the question (to the information technology group), and wait–perhaps after the nightly sales are processed (maybe 24 hours later), and finally, we receive an answer. This is a business model that doesn't hold up now with the many new sources of data (such as social media or mobile applications), which record and capture data in real time, all of the time. The answers to the questions asked may actually change within a 24-hour period (such is the case with trending now information that you may have observed when you are online).

Given the industry hot topics such as **Internet of Things (IoT)**, it is safe to say that these pace expectations will only quicken.

Variety

Thinking back to our previous mention of relational databases, it is generally accepted that relational databases are considered to be highly structured, although they may contain text in VCHAR, CLOB, or BLOB fields.

Data today (and especially when we talk about big data) comes from many kinds of data sources, and the level in which that data is structured varies greatly from data source to data source. In fact, the growing trend is for data to continue to lose structure and to continue to add hundreds (or more?) of new formats and structures (formats that go beyond pure text, photo, audio, video, web, GPS data, sensor data, relational databases, documents, SMS, pdf, flash, and so on) all of the time.

Categorization

The process of categorization helps us to gain an understanding of the data source.

The industry commonly categorizes big data this way–into the two groups (structured and unstructured)–but the categorizing doesn't stop there.

Some simple research reveals some interesting new terms for subcategorizing these two types of data varieties:

Structured data includes subcategories such as created, provoked, transactional, compiled, and experimental, while unstructured data includes subcategories such as captured and submitted (just to name a few of the currently trending terms for categorizing the types of big data. You may be familiar with or be able to find more).

It's worth taking some time here to speak about these various data formats (varieties) to help drive the point to the reader of the challenges of dealing with the numerous big data varieties:

1. **Created data**: This is the data being created for a purpose; such as focus group surveys or asking website users to establish an account on the site (rather than allowing anonymous access).
2. **Provoked data**: This is described as data received after some form of provoking, perhaps such as providing someone with the opportunity to express the individual's personal view on a topic, such as customers filling out product review forms.

3. **Transactional data**: This is data that is described as database transactions, for example, the record of a sales transaction.

4. **Compiled data**: This is data described as information collected (or compiled) on a particular topic such as credit scores.

5. **Experimental data**: This is described as when someone experiments with data and/or sources of data to explore potential new insights. For example, combining or relating sales transactions to marketing and promotional information to determine a (potential) correlation.

6. **Captured data**: This is the data created passively due to a person's behavior (like when you enter a search term on Google, perhaps the creepiest data of all!).

7. **User-generated data**: This is the data generated every second by individuals, such as from Twitter, Facebook, YouTube, and so on (compared to captured data, this is data you willingly create or put out there).

To sum up, big data comes with no common or expected format and the time required to impose a structure on the data has proven to be no longer worth it.

Such are the 3Vs

In addition to what we mentioned earlier, there are additional challenging areas that big data brings to the table especially to the task of data visualization, for example, the ability to effectively deal with data quality, outliers, and to display results in a meaningful way, to name a few.

Again, it's worth quickly visiting each of these topics here now.

Data quality

The value of almost anything and everything is directly proportional to its level of quality and higher quality is equal to higher value.

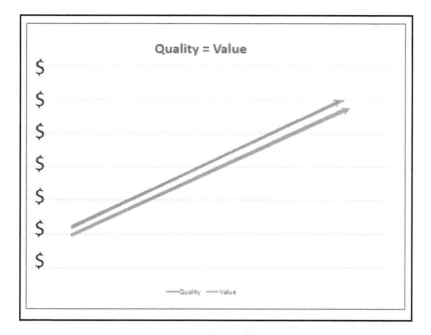

Data is no different. Data (any data) can only prove to be a valuable instrument if its quality is certain.

The general areas of data quality include:

- Accuracy
- Completeness
- Update status
- Relevance
- Consistency (across sources)
- Reliability
- Appropriateness
- Accessibility

The quality of data can be affected by the way it is entered, stored, and managed and the process of addressing data quality (referred to most often as quality assurance, **data quality assurance (DQA)**, requires a routine and regular review and evaluation of the data, and performing on going processes termed profiling and scrubbing (this is vital even if the data is stored in multiple disparate systems making these processes difficult).

Effective profiling and scrubbing of data necessitates the use of flexible, efficient techniques capable of handling complex quality issues hidden deep in the depths of very large and ever accumulating (big data) datasets.

With the complexities of big data (and its levels of volume, velocity, and variety), it should be easy for one to recognize how problematic and restrictive the DQA process is and will continue to become.

Dealing with outliers

The following is a simple figure introducing the concept of an outlier, that is, one lonesome red dot separated from the group:

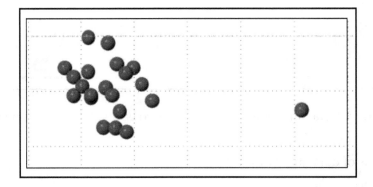

As per Sham Mustafa, founder and CEO of data scientist marketplace Correlation One:

> *"Anyone who is trying to interpret data needs to care about outliers. It doesn't matter if the data is financial, sociological, medical, or even qualitative. Any analysis of that data or information must consider the presence and effect of outliers. Outliers (data that is "distant" from the rest of the data) indicating variabilities or errors – need to be identified and dealt with."*

For clarification, you might accept the notion that an outlier is an observation point that is distant or vastly different from other observations (or data points) in a sum of data.

Once identified, regularly accepted methods for dealing with these outliers may be (simply?) moving them to another file or replacing the outliers with other more reasonable or appropriate values. This way of outlier processing is perhaps not such a complicated process, but is one that must be seriously thought out and rethought before introducing any process to identify and address outliers in a petabyte or more of data.

Another point to consider is, are the outliers you identify in your data an indicator that the data itself is bad or faulty or are the outliers' random variations caused by new and interesting points or characteristics within your data?

Either way, the presence of outliers in your data will require a valid and (especially in the case of big data) a robust method for dealing with them.

Meaningful displays

Rather than words or text, the following diagram clearly demonstrates the power of a visualization when conveying information:

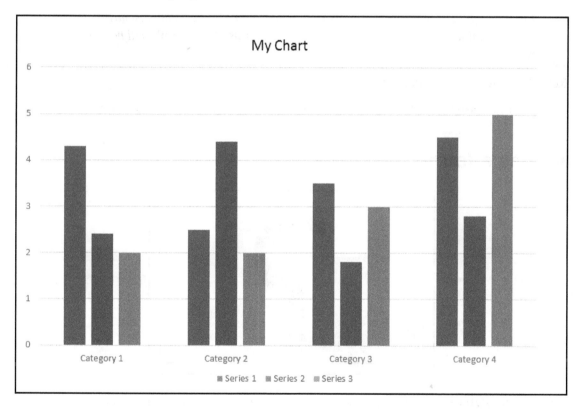

A picture is worth a thousand words and *Seeing is believing* are just two adages that elucidate the powers of data visualization.

As per Millman/Miller Data Visualization: Getting Value from Information 2014:

> *"The whole point of data visualization is to provide a visual experience."*

Successfully conducting business today requires that organizations tap into all the available data stores finding and analyzing relevant information very quickly, looking for indications and insights.

Data visualization is a key technique permitting individuals to perform analysis, identify key trends or events, and make more confident decisions much more quickly. In fact, data visualization has been referred to as the visual representation of business intelligence and industry research analyst Lyndsay Wise said in an article back in 2013:

> *"Even though there is plenty that users can accomplish now using data visualization, the reality is that we are just at the tip of the iceberg in terms of how people will be using this technology in the future."*

Refer to the following link for more information:

```
https://tdwi.org/articles/2013/04/02/Data-Visualization-Boosts-BI-Value.aspx
```

Adding a fourth V

The idea of establishing and improving the quality levels of big data might also be classified as the fourth V: veracity. Data that is disparate, large, multiformatted, and quick to accumulate and/or change (also known as big data) causes uncertainty and doubt (can I trust this data?). The uncertainty that comes with big data may cause the perhaps valuable data to be excluded or over looked.

As we've already mentioned, big data visualization forces a rethinking of the massive amounts of both structured and unstructured data (at great velocity) and unstructured data will always contain a certain amount of uncertain and imprecise data. Social media data, for example, is characteristically uncertain.

A method for dealing with big data veracity is by assigning a veracity grade or veracity score for specific datasets to evade making decisions based on analysis of uncertain and imprecise big data.

Although big data may well offer businesses exponentially more opportunities for visualizing their data into actionable insights, it also increases the required effort and expertise to do so (successfully and effectively).

Again, the same challenges are presented; such as accessing the level of detail needed from perhaps unimaginable volumes of levels of data, in an ever-growing variety of different formats–all at a very high speed–is noticeably difficult.

Visualization philosophies

A meaningful display requires you to pay attention to various proven practice philosophies; these concepts include (but are not limited to):

- The proper arrangement of related information
- Appropriately using color(s)
- Correctly defining decimal placements
- Limiting the use of 3D effects or ornate gauge designs

The reader should take note that this book is not intending to cover all of the fundamental data visualization techniques, but is focusing on the challenges of big data visualization practices and it is assumed that the reader has general knowledge of and experience with the process of data visualization. However, one who may be interested in the topic should perhaps take some time to review the idea of the *Data-Ink Ratio* introduced by *Edward Tufte*. Tufte does an excellent job in introducing and explaining this concept in the best-selling book *The Visual Display of Quantitative Information, Edward R. Tufte*, January 2001.

More on variety

Without context, data is meaningless and the same applies to visual displays (or visualizations) of that data.

For example, data sourced from social media may present entirely different insights depending on user demographics (that is, age group, sex, or income bracket), platform (that is, Facebook or Twitter), or audience (those who intend to consume the visualizations).

Acquiring a proper understanding (establishing a context) of the data takes significant domain expertise as well as the ability to properly analyze the data; big data certainty complicates these practices with its seemingly endless number of formats and varieties of both structured and unstructured data.

Velocity

Even if you are able to assign the appropriate context to your data, the usability or value of the data will be (at least) reduced if the data is not timely. The effort and expense required to source, understand, and visualize data is squandered if the results are stale, obsolete, or potentially invalid by the time the data is available to the intended consumers. For example, when a state government agency is preparing a budget request for the governor, the most up-to-date consensus figures are vital; without accuracy, here, the funds may fall short of the actual needs.

The challenge of speedily crunching numbers exists within any data analysis, but when considering the varieties and volumes of data involved in big data projects, it becomes even more evident.

Volume

It may (or may not) be evident to the reader that too much information displayed in one place can cause the viewer to have what is referred to as sensory overload and that simple restrictions such as real estate (the available viewing space on a web page or monitor) can (and most likely will) be detrimental to the value of a visualization trying to depict too many data points or metrics.

In addition, complicated or intricate visuals or those that attempt to aggregate or otherwise source a large number of data sources most likely will be hindered by the experience of slow performance. In other words, the more data you need to process to create or refresh your visualization, the longer wait time there will most likely be, which will increase audience frustration levels and usability and value of the visualization.

Beyond the earlier mentioned pitfalls, when dealing with big data, even creating a simple bar graph visualization can be overwhelmingly difficult since attempting to plot points for analysis with extremely large amounts of information or a large variety of categories of information simply won't work.

Visualizations of data should be used to uncover trends and spot outliers much quicker than using worksheets or reports containing columns and rows of numbers and text, but these opportunities will be lost if care is not taken to address the mentioned challenges.

Users can leverage visualizations such as a column chart, for example, to see where sales may be headed or to identify topics that need attention at a glance or glimpse. But imagine trying to churn through and chart twenty billion records of data! Even if the data could be processed into a visualization, anyone trying to view that number of plots within a single visualization will have a very difficult time just viewing so many data points.

All is not lost

Thankfully, there are various approaches (or strategies) that have come to exist and can be used for preparing effective big data visualizations as well as addressing the hindrances we've mentioned (variety, velocity, volume, and veracity).

Some of the examples include:

- You can change the type of the visualization, for example, switching from a column graph to a line chart can allow you to handle more data points within the visualization.
- You can use higher-level clustering. In other words, you can create larger, broader stroke groupings of the data to be represented in the visualization (with perhaps linked subcharts or popups allowing a selected grouping to be broken out into subgroupings) rather than trying to visualize an excessive number of groups.
- You can remove outliers from the visualization. Outliers typically represent less than 5 percent of a data source, but when you're working with massive amounts of data, viewing that 5 percent of the data is challenging. Outliers can be removed and if appropriate, be presented in a separate data visualization.
- You can consider capping, which means setting a threshold for the data you will allow into your visualization. This cuts down on the range or data making for a smaller, more focused image.

These strategies (and others) help, but aren't really sufficient when it comes to working with big data.

The remaining chapters of this book are outlined later in this chapter and I will provide practical approaches and solutions (with examples) to consider for successful big data visualization.

Approaches to big data visualization

When it comes to the topic of big data, simple data visualization tools with their basic features become somewhat inadequate. The concepts and models necessary to efficiently and effectively visualize big data can be daunting, but are not unobtainable.

Using workable approaches (studied in the following chapters of this book) the reader will review some of the most popular (or currently trending) tools, such as:

- Hadoop
- R
- Data Manager
- D3
- Tableau
- Python
- Splunk

This is done in an effort to meet the challenges of big data visualization and support better decision making.

It is expected that our reading audience would be data analysts or those having at least basic knowledge of data analysis and visualization and now are interested in learning about the various alternatives for big data visualization in order to make their analysis more useful, more valuable, and hopefully have some fun doing it!

Readers holding some knowledge of big data platform tools (such as Hadoop) and having exposure to programming languages (such as perhaps R or Python) will make the most of the remaining chapters, but all should benefit.

Access, speed, and storage

We've already touched on the 3Vs (plus veracity), which include the challenges of both the storing of the large and ever-growing amounts (volumes) of data as well as being able to rapidly (with velocity) access, manipulate, and manage that data.

`Chapter 2`, *Access, Speed, and Storage with Hadoop*, of this book will expound on this topic and introduce Hadoop as the game changing technology to use for this purpose.

Dealing with expanding data sizes may lead to perpetually expanding a machines resources, to cover the expanding size of the data. Typically, this is a short-lived solution.

When dealing with data too large to handle with a single machine's memory (that is, big data) a common approach is to sample the data, meaning that basically you try to construct a smaller dataset from the full dataset that you feel is reasonably representative (of the full dataset). Using Hadoop, you have the ability to run many exploratory data analysis tasks on full datasets, without sampling, with the results efficiently returned to your machine or laptop.

Entering Hadoop

Hadoop removes the restrictions and limitations that hardware levies on the storage of big data by providing the ability to streamline data (from every touch point in any organizational data source, whether the data is structured or unstructured) for your needs across clusters of computers (which means this solution is basically infinitely scalable) using simple programming models.

The Hadoop online product documentation points out:

> *"Data which was previously too expensive to store, can now be stored and made available for analysis to improve business insights at 1/10 to 1/50 the cost on a per terabyte basis."*

Refer to the following link for more information www.mapr.com/why-hadoop/game-changer2016.

We'll cover working examples to demonstrate solutions for effectively storing and accessing big data, but the reader should take note that Hadoop also works well with smaller amounts of data (as well as the infinity large amounts) so you can be sure that any example used in this book will not have to be reworked based upon the actual size (or actual volume) of data you may be using in your future analysis projects.

In an effort to paint a complete picture here (and we'll do this throughout all of the chapters), we will also take some time and consider the how and why of non-Hadoop (or alternate) solutions to the examples given–and considering how well they may compare to a Hadoop solution.

Context

When it comes to performing data analytics, facts can be stupid and stubborn things. They can provide us with the business intelligence metrics we long for, but without predictive analytics based on contextual interpretation, we may find ourselves using skewed quantitative analysis that produces less-than-desirable results.

 The appropriate use of context in analytics makes all the difference toward achieving optimal results, a Business@American staff article, which is available at https://onlinebusiness.american.edu/how-do-we-use-data-for-good-add-context/.

In Chapter 3, *Context – Understanding Your Data Using R*, of this book, the importance of gaining an understanding of the data you are working with and specifically, the challenges of establishing or adding context to big data will be covered with working examples demonstrating solutions for effectively addressing the issues that are presented.

Adding context to data requires manipulation of that data to review and perhaps reformat, adding calculations, aggregations, or additional columns or re-ordering, and so on.

In Chapter 3, *Context – Understanding Your Data Using R*, we will introduce the R programming tool as the choice for performing this type of processing and manipulating your data.

R is a language and environment very focused on statistical computing.

R provides a wide variety of statistical (linear and nonlinear modeling, classical statistical tests, time-series analysis, classification, clustering, and so on) and graphical techniques, and it is highly extensible. You can refer to more information on this at www.r-project.org/about.html.

Beyond the perhaps more sophisticated modeling techniques such as performing a time-series analysis, R also supports the need for performing simple tasks such as creating a summary table, which can be used to determine data groupings.

One thing to keep in mind is that R preserves everything in machine memory.

This can become a problem if you are working with big data (even with the introduction of the low resource costs of today).

With R, sampling is a popular method for dealing with big data. In Chapter 3, *Context – Understanding Your Data Using R*, our focus is on gaining context of data, so sampling is acceptable.

R is great for manipulating and cleaning data, producing probability statistics, as well as actually creating visualizations with data, so it's a good choice for establishing a context for your data.

Quality

It has been said that beauty is in the eyes of the beholder, and the same can be said when trying to define data quality. What this means is if the data meets your level of expectations or, at least the minimal of requirements of a particular project, then it has some form or level of quality.

Data can have acceptable quality even if there are known complications with it. These complications can be overcome with processes we'll discuss later or, if appropriate, simply overlooked.

Even though your data may contain acceptable complications, the reader should be sure to make no mistake such that any data visualization created based upon this data will only prove to be a valuable tool if the quality of that data is assured to be at the level required. However, when using large volumes of data, it can become extremely difficult to address the quality of the data.

There are many examples of the effects of poor data quality, such as the following, which was written in an article by Sean Jackson (`http://www.actian.com/about-us/blog/never-underestimate-importance-good-data-quality/`):

> *"A business professional could not understand why response rates to campaigns and activities were so low. Nor why they couldn't really use analytics to get any competitive advantage. A quick investigation of their data and systems soon showed that a large section of the data they were using was either out-of-date, badly formatted, or just erroneous."*

Data quality solutions must enable you to clean, manage, and make reliable data available across your organization.

Chapter 4, *Addressing Big Data Quality*, of this book offers working examples demonstrating solutions for effectively assessing and improving the level of quality of big data sources.

Typically, the first step in determining the quality of your data is performing a process referred to as profiling the data (mentioned earlier in this chapter). This is sort of an overall auditing process that helps you examine and determine whether your existing data sources meet the quality expectations or perhaps standards of your intended use or purpose.

Profiling is vitally important in that it can help you identify concerns that may exist within the data that attending to up front (before going on and actually creating a data visualization) will save valuable time (rather than having to process and reprocess the poor qualities of the data later). In fact, more importantly, it can save you from creating and presenting a visualization that contains an inaccurate view of the data.

Data profiling becomes even more critical when working with perhaps unstructured raw data sources (or data that is a mix of structured and unstructured data) that do not have referential integrity or any other quality controls. In addition, single source (data sourced from only a single place) and multisource data (a dataset that is sourced from more than one place) will most likely have additional opportunities for data concerns.

Concerns found in single sources are typically intensified when multiple sources need to be integrated into one dataset for a project. Each source may contain data concerns, but in addition, the same data in different data sources may be represented differently, overlap, or contradict.

Typical profiling tasks include the following:

- Identifying fields/columns within the data
- Listing field/column attributes and statistics such as column lengths and value distribution percentages
- Reviewing field/column value distributions
- Null ratios
- Reporting of value statistics such as minimum, maximum, average, and standard deviation for numeric columns, and minimum and maximum for date and time columns
- Identifying all the distinct values in the data
- Identifying patterns and pattern distributions within the data

The goal of these tasks (and others) is to (as the name implies) establish your data's profile by determining its characteristics, relationships, and patterns within the data and, hopefully, produce a clearer view of the content and quality of your data, that is, the data profile.

After profiling, one would most likely proceed with performing some form of scrubbing (also sometimes referred to as cleansing or in some cases preparing) of the data (to improve its quality, also mentioned earlier in this chapter).

The processes of cleansing data may be somewhat or even entirely different, depending upon the data's intended use. Because of this, the task of defining what is to be determined an error is the critical first step to be performed before any processing of the data. Even what is done to resolve the defined errors may differ, again based upon the data's intended use.

During the process of cleansing or scrubbing your data, you would perform tasks such as perhaps reformatting fields or adding missing values, and so on.

Generally, scrubbing is made up of the following efforts:

- Defining and determining errors within the data–what do you consider an error?
- Searching and identifying error instances–once an error is defined, where do they exist in your data?
- Correction of the errors–remove them or update them to acceptable values.
- Error instance and document error types–or labeling (how was the error determined and what was done to resolve it).
- Updating the entry mechanism to avoid future errors–create a process to make sure future occurrences of this type are dealt with.

In `Chapter 4`, *Addressing Big Data Quality*, we've elected to continue (from the previous chapter) to leverage the *R* programming language to accomplish some of the profiling work and also introduce and use the open source data manager utility for manipulating our data and addressing the quality.

Data manager is an excellent utility available as a library of Java code that is aimed at data synchronization work for moving data between different locations and different databases.

Displaying results

Data visualization is when you manually or otherwise organize and display data in a pictorial or graphic format in an attempt to enable your audience to:

- See the results of your analysis efforts more clearly
- Simplify the complexities within the data you are using
- Understand and grasp a point that you are using the data to make

Not a new concept

This concept of using pictures–typography, color, contrast, and shape–to communicate or understand data is not new and has been around for literally centuries, from the manual creation of maps and graphs in the 17th century to the invention of the pie chart in the early 1800s.

Today, computers can be used to process large amounts of data lightning fast to make visualizations tremendously more valuable. Going forward, we can expect the data visualization process to continue to evolve, perhaps as more of a mixture of art and science rather than a numbers crunching technology.

Instant gratifications

An exciting example of the data visualization evolutionary process is how the industry has moved data visualizations past the process of generating and publishing charts and graphs for an audience to review and deliberate on to now having set up an expectation for interactive visualizations.

With interactive visualization, we can take the concept of data visualization much, much further by using technology to allow the audience to interact with the data; giving the user the self-service ability to drill down into the generated pictures, charts, and graphs (to access more or specific details), interactively in real time (or near real time) to change what data is displayed (perhaps a different time frame or event) and how it's processed and/or presented (maybe select a bar graph rather than a pie chart).

This allows visualizations to be much more effective and personalized.

In Chapter 5, *Displaying Results with D3*, we will go through the topic of displaying the results of analysis on big data using a typical web browser using **Data Driven Documents (D3)** in a variety of examples. D3 allows the ability to apply prebuilt data visualizations to datasets.

Data-driven documents

Data Driven Documents is referred within the open community as D3.

D3 is an open source library written in JavaScript. The objective is to allow for easily manipulating documents based upon data using standard web browsing technologies (such as HTML or CSS). Its value-add is to provide you with full capabilities without having to build your own or strapping yourself to some proprietary framework.

These library components give you excellent tools for big data visualization and a data-driven approach to DOM manipulation. D3's functional style allows the reuse of library code modules that you've already built (or others have already built) adding pretty much any particular features you need or want (or don't want) to. This creates a means that can become as powerful as you want it (or have the time to make it) to be, to give a unique style to your data visualizations, manipulate and make it all interactive–exactly how you want or need it to be.

Dashboards

As discussed earlier in this chapter, big data is collecting and accumulating daily, in fact; minute-by-minute and there is a realization that organizations rely on this information for a variety of reasons.

Various types of reporting formats are utilized on this data, including data dashboards.

As with everything, there are various apprehensions as to the most accurate definition of what a data dashboard is.

For example, A. Chiang writes:

> *"A dashboard is a visual display of the most important information needed to achieve one or more objectives; consolidated and arranged on a single screen so the information can be monitored at a glance."*

Refer to the following link for more information:
`http://www.dashboardinsight.com/articles/digital-dashboards/fundamentals/what-i s-a-dashboard.aspx.`

Whatever the definition, any dashboard has the capacity for supplying timely, important information for its audience to use in decision making, if it is well designed and constructed.

It is critical that dashboards present data in a relevant, concise, and well-thought-out manner (not just a collection of visual representations in a workbook or spreadsheet) and in addition, dashboards have to have a supporting infrastructure capable of refreshing the dashboard in a well-timed manner as well as including some form of DQA. Making decisions based upon a dashboard with incorrectly presented, stale, or even incorrect data can lead to disaster.

Chapter 6, *Dashboard for Big Data – Tableau*, of this book offers examination of the topic of effective dashboarding and includes working examples demonstrating solutions for effectively presenting results based upon your big data analysis in a real-time dashboard format using Tableau.

Tableau is categorized as business intelligence software designed to help people see and understand data; more than just a code library, Tableau is considered to be a suite or a family of interactive data visualization products.

Tableau's structure allows us the ability to combine multiple views of data from multiple sources into a single, highly effective dashboard that can provide the data consumers with much richer insights. Tableau also works with a variety of formats of (both structured and unstructured) data and can handle the volumes of big data, literally, petabytes or terabytes, millions or billions of rows, turning that big data into valuable visualizations for targeted audiences.

To address the velocity of today's big data world, you can use Tableau to connect directly to local and cloud data sources, or just import your data for fast in-memory (more on in-memory later in this book) performance.

Another goal of Tableau is self-service analytics (which we mentioned earlier in this chapter and will talk more about later on), where a user can have a dialog with selected data to ask questions (in real time, not in a batch mode) using easy point-and-click analytics to mine big data intuitively and effectively discovering understandings and opportunities that may exist within the dataset or datasets.

Some of the more exciting abilities Tableau offers include:

- Real-time drag-and-drop cluster analysis
- Cross data source joining
- Powerful data connectors
- Mobile enabled
- Real-time territory or region data exploration

Outliers

In Chapter 7, *Dealing with Outliers Using Python*, we will dive into Outliers.

As was defined earlier in this chapter, an outlier is an observation point that is distant or vastly different from the other observed data points within the data.

Although outliers typically represent (only) about 1 to 5 percent of your data, when you're working with big data, investigating, or even just viewing, 1 to 5 percent of that data is rather difficult.

Investigation and adjudication

Outliers, you see, can be determined to be noninfluential or very influential to the point you are trying to make with your data visualization.

The act or process of making this determination is critically important to your analysis, but it is also very problematic when dealing with the larger volumes, many varieties, and velocities of big data. For example, a fundamental step to help make this determination is called the sizing of your samples, which is the main mathematical process of calculating the percentage of outliers to the size of the data sample, which is not so simple a task when the data is in petabytes or terabytes!

Identifying and removing outliers can be tremendously complicated and there are many differences in opinions as to how to go about determining the percentage of outliers that exist in your dataset as well as determining their effect on the data and deciding what to do with them. It is, however, generally accepted that an automated process can be created that can facilitate at least the identification of outliers, possibly even through the use of visualization.

Carrying on, all the approaches for the investigation and adjudication of outliers such as sorting, capping, graphing, and so on require manipulating and processing of the data using a tool that is feature–rich and robust.

This chapter offers working examples demonstrating solutions for effectively and efficiently identifying and dealing with big data outliers (as well as some other dataset anomalies) using Python.

Python is a scripting language that is extremely easy to learn and incredibly readable, since its coding syntax so closely resembles the English language.

According to the article, *The 9 most in-demand programming languages of 2016*, by *Bouwkamp*, available at
`http://www.codingdojo.com/blog/9-most-in-demand-programming-languages-of-2016`,
Python is listed in the top most in-demand programming languages (at the time of writing).

Born as far back as 1989 and created by *Guido van Rossum*, Python is actually very simple in nature, but it is also considered by the industry to be extremely powerful, fast, and it can be run in almost any environment.

As per `www.python.org`:

> *"Open sourced (and free!), Python is part of the winning formula for productivity, software quality, and maintainability at many companies and institutions around the world."*

There is a growing interest within the industry to utilize the Python language for data analysis and even for big data analysis and it is the exceptional choice for the data scientist to perform typical day to day activities as it provides libraries, in fact a standard library (even some focusing specifically on big data, such as Pydoop and SciPy) to accomplish almost anything you need or want to do with the data you have or are accumulating, including:

- Automations
- Building websites and web pages
- Accessing and manipulating data
- Calculating statistics
- Creating visualizations
- Reporting
- Building predictive and explanatory models
- Evaluating models on additional data
- Integrating models into production systems

As a final note here, Python's standard library is very extensive, offering a wide range of built-in modules that provide access to system functionalities, as well as standardized solutions to solve many problems that occur in everyday programming making this an obvious choice to explore for dealing with big data outliers and related processing.

Operational intelligence

In `Chapter 8`, *Big Data Operational Intelligence with Splunk*, of this book, we concentrate on big data Operational Intelligence.

Operational intelligence (OI) is a type of analytics that attempts to deliver visibility and insight from (usually machine generated) operational or event data, running queries against streaming data feeds in real time, producing analytic results as operational instructions, which can be immediately acted upon by an organization, through manual or automated actions (a clear example of turning datasets into value!).

Sophisticated OI systems also provide the ability to associate metadata with certain metrics, process steps, channels, and so on, found within data. With this ability, it becomes easy to acquire additional related information, for example, machine-generated operational data is typically full of unique identifiers and result or status codes. These codes or identifiers may be efficient for processing and storage, but are not always easily interpreted by human beings. To make this data more readable (and therefore more valuable) we can associate additional information that is more user friendly with the data results–possibly in the form of a status or event description or perhaps a product name or machine name.

Once there is an understanding of the challenges of applying basic analytics and visualization techniques to operational big data, the value of that data can be better or more quickly realized. In this chapter, we offer working examples demonstrating solutions for the valuing of operational or event big data with operational intelligence using Splunk.

So, what is Splunk? H. Klein says:

> *"Splunk started out as a kind of "Google for Log files". It does a lot more... It stores all your logs and provides very fast search capabilities roughly in the same way Google does for the internet..." — https://helgeklein.com/blog/2014/09/splunk-work/*

Splunk software is a great tool to help unlock hidden value in machine generated, operational data (as well as other types of data). With Splunk, you can collect, index, search, analyze, and visualize all your data in one place, providing an integrated method to organize and extract real-time insights from massive amounts of (big data) machine data from virtually anywhere.

Splunk stores data in flat files, assigning indexes to the files. Splunk doesn't require any database software running in the background to make this happen. Splunk calls these files indexers. Splunk can index any type of time-series data (data with timestamps), making it an optimal choice for big data OI solutions. During data indexing, Splunk breaks data into events based on the timestamps it identifies.

Although using simple search terms will work, (for example, a machine ID) Splunk also offers its own **Search Processing Language** (**SPL**). Splunk SPL (think of it as kind of like SQL) is an extremely powerful tool for searching enormous amounts of big data and performing statistical operations on what is relevant within a specific context.

There are multiple versions of Splunk, including a free version that is pretty much fully functional.

Summary

In this chapter, we were offered an explanation of just what the term data visualization means and discussed the industry accepted conventional visualization concepts.

In addition, we introduced the challenges of working with big data and outlined the topics and technologies that the rest of this book will present.

In the next chapter, we address volume, speed, and velocity using Hadoop.

2
Access, Speed, and Storage with Hadoop

This chapter aims to target the challenge of storing and accessing large volumes and varieties (structured or unstructured) of data offering working examples demonstrating solutions for effectively addressing these issues.

Since it is expected that you are somewhat familiar with Hadoop, this chapter starts with a brief overview of the technology, but doesn't intend to cover all of the details as the goal is to provide a demonstration using Hadoop as a technology to address the challenge of storing and accessing big data.

In addition, in an effort towards completeness, we'll touch on the possible alternatives to using Hadoop, such as Apache Spark and even a simple scripting solution.

By the end of this chapter, the reader should have an idea of what Hadoop is and how it works, should have acquired an appreciation for the reasoning for leveraging Hadoop to store, and should have accessed big data and also have worked through example solutions using Hadoop.

We'll break down this chapter like this:

- About Hadoop
- Log files and Excel
- Hadoop and big data
- Example 1
- Example 2

About Hadoop

Let's start out with an explanation of Hadoop that is generally circulated.

As per Apache Hadoop wikipedia.org, 2016:

> *"Hadoop is an open-source software "framework" for distributed storage and distributed processing (of very large datasets) on computer clusters built from commodity hardware."*

The following is a visualization that may help understand the master-to-slave architecture used by Hadoop:

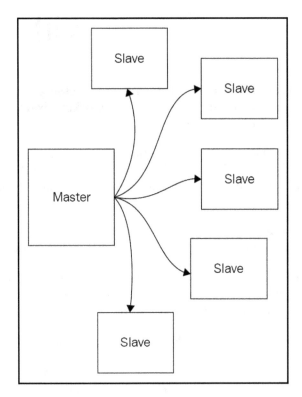

Hadoop uses an architecture called **MapReduce**. This is a design that designates a processor (in a cluster of processors) as the master, which controls distributing or mapping tasks to other slave processors to process your data, thus reducing the processing performed by the cluster of processors to a single output result. So, you can now see that the name mapped reduction or MapReduce (of processing tasks) makes sense.

Hadoop is able to take your data and split it up (or distribute it) over a number of computers that have space or resources available.

These computers need not be high-end, overcapable devices (that is, they can be easily available, average machines that are therefore called commodities), they just need to be named as part of a group or cluster available to the Hadoop framework. That's the first part of the magic, the other side of Hadoop is that it keeps track of where every file was placed and is able to make it all available (seemingly as one coherent database) with minimal response time. It is important to note that simply scattering files of data about isn't all that clever; what is clever is that Hadoop is capable of knowing which computers are closest to the data it wants to access at any time. This vastly cuts down on network traffic that would be caused by searching for specific data when needed (that is, now where did I put that file?).

Hadoop FAQs (Hadoop, `WhatIs.com` Rouse 2015) include:

- Hadoop is free
- Hadoop is Java-based
- Hadoop was initially released in 2011
- Hadoop is part of the Apache project sponsored by the **Apache Software Foundation (ASF)**
- Hadoop was inspired by Google's MapReduce, a software framework in which an application is broken down into numerous small parts
- Hadoop was named after its creator's (Doug Cutting) child's stuffed toy elephant
- Hadoop consists of the Hadoop kernel, MapReduce, the **Hadoop Distributed File System (HDFS)**, and a number of related projects such as Apache Hive, HBase, and Zookeeper
- The Hadoop framework is used by major players, including Google, Yahoo, and IBM, largely for applications involving search engines and advertising
- The preferred operating systems are Windows and Linux, but Hadoop can also work with BSD and OS X

Certainly, there are many more interesting Hadoop FAQs, but I'm sure that you get the picture, so let's move on.

What else but Hadoop?

Is Hadoop the only choice for storing and processing your big data?

You'll perhaps find that Hadoop is the tool that is most known for handling big data. In fact, there are misconceptions with some that when talking about big data, you're talking about Hadoop or, if discussing Hadoop, you're discussing big data.

Obviously, that notion is incorrect.

In fact, there are a number of alternatives to using Hadoop and some are gaining popularity every day. There are (as with any technology choice) both pros and cons with choosing to implement Hadoop and those (among other reasons) are driving the interest in other options.

Two popular alternatives to Hadoop are Apache Spark and Cluster MapReduce.

Apache Spark is open source (like Hadoop), runs in-memory, and promises faster speed than Hadoop and offers unique **application programming interface (API)**. Cluster MapReduce was developed on top of the Hadoop MapReduce framework concepts by an online ad company that was using Hadoop but wanted more. Compared to Hadoop, Cluster MapReduce supposedly offers a more efficient solution that:

- Uses more straightforward creation of data queries
- Has a lighter footprint
- Has greater ability to be customized
- Has more resilience to failures

IBM too!

It would be prudent to take a moment here to consider IBM's enterprise version of Hadoop.

IBM has taken the Hadoop concepts and created their own version of a Hadoop-like platform (IBM Open Platform) for big data projects using the most current Apache Hadoop open source content. This is offered as a free download and (as one would expect) there is also a paid support offering, should you be interested (perhaps in an effort to instill confidence in an organization considering developing with an open source tool?).

In addition, IBM offers the *IBM BigInsights Quick Start* edition, which combines their open platform with what they are calling *enterprise-grade* features for data visualization (and advanced analytics) projects.

 You can review this at:
`www.ibm.com/analytics/us/en/technology/hadoop`.

So, there really are other options (rather than using Hadoop) and more will come.

Hadoop is, without question, extremely powerful, but it uses complex methods for moving data and isn't all that efficient when dealing with unstructured data (a data type increasingly prevalent today). Given the new options, the aforementioned automatic association of big data and Hadoop is becoming less observed.

In this book, we are using Hadoop, but those who deal with big data or unstructured data would be judicious to scope out all the available options (including simple scripting alternatives) when considering their own needs.

Part of any project decision making process is getting intimate with the detailed requirements. On the topic of data visualization, it is imperative to know your data intimately. One big decision to make first is, does your data really qualify as big data?

In an article named *The Big Data Conundrum: How to Define it?* by Stuart Ward, he writes:

> "Some organizations point out that large datasets are not always complex and small datasets are not always simple. Their point is that the complexity of a dataset is an important factor in deciding whether it is "big."

An interesting point here is data that is overly complex in nature can be considered big data and require the big data mindset (even though you may not be dealing with large volumes of data).

Before getting started with Hadoop and our Hadoop example use cases, let's take a few moments to consider a simpler solution, such as simple data file processing with a scripting language.

Log files and Excel

Let's consider a somewhat realistic use case where you have been provided a number of modified web log files that you want to create some visualizations from.

In Chapter 4, *Addressing Big Data Quality*, we will discuss data profiling (in regards to data quality), but for now, we'll assume that we know the following about our data files:

- The files are of various sizes and somewhat unstructured.
- The data in the files contain information logged by Internet users.
- The data includes such things as computer IP addresses, a date, timestamp, and a web address/URL. There is more information in the files, but for our exercise here we really just want to create a graphical representation showing the number of times each web address was hit during each month (there are actually software packages that provide web statistics, but we'll suppose you don't have access to any of them).

The following is a sample transaction (record) from one of our files:

```
221.738.236 - - [15/Oct/2014:6:55:2] GET
/cart.do?action=view&itemId=EST-6&productId=SC-MG-
G10&JSESSIONID=SD5SL9FF2ADFF4958 HTTP 1.12002334
http://www.rpropgramming.com
```

One's first inclination might be to load up the files into Microsoft Excel, do some pivoting and filtering, and then prepare some Excel graphs, but these files exceed the capacity of the tool (refer to the following screenshot):

Your next thought might be: big data and head for Hadoop.

Realistically though, although the files are too big for Excel to handle, we are able to manipulate them using our standard business issue laptop (although, perhaps, a bit slowly) and even though there are several files we need our data visualization to source from, it still is manageable. So, this exercise really doesn't qualify as big data, based upon volume. The data is a bit unstructured, but (notice the sample transactions) they are not at all complicated or propose a variety constraint.

Finally, for this particular exercise, the files to be used are historic (based upon a previous period of time), so we don't have to worry about velocity. Again, this is not a big data project (although, later in this section, we see how it will grow into one).

So, a rudimental solution option is to use the power of R to manipulate all of the files and create some simple visualizations based upon content.

For this example, I won't be explaining the details of the R scripts used, I just want to prove the point that R can be used to create interesting visualizations with data files too large for MS Excel. I have included my scripts here for completeness, however, you need to make a note that the R scripts shown here work, but were created quickly in an ad hoc fashion using the R console for MS Windows and most likely are not the most efficient in style. We will take more time to understand R in Chapter 3, *Understanding Your Data Using R*.

An R scripting example

My first step was to combine (or bind) my log files into a single comma delimited text file.

This is simply done in R using the rbind() function:

```
complete.dat <- rbind(C:/Big Data Visualization/weblog1.txt,C:/Big Data
Visualization/weblog2.txt)
datafile1 <- read.csv("C:/Big Data Visualization/weblog1.txt", header=T,
sep=",")
datafile2 <- read.csv("C:/Big Data Visualization/weblog2.txt", header=T,
sep=",")
datafile <- rbind(datafile1, datafile2)
write.csv(datafile,"C:/Big Data Visualization/oneWebLog.txt")
```

Once I had a single (big!) file, I wanted to pull out only the information I want to use for my visualization, so again I used a simple R script to create another text file that contains only two columns: the date (actually just the month name) and a web address. You can see that the data and web address are in columns four and nine, respectively. Note that our weblog files are separated only by spaces:

```
tmpRTable<-read.table("C:/Big Data Visualization/oneWebLog.txt")
tmpRTable<-tmpRTable,c(4,9)]
data.df <- data.frame(tmpRTable)
adata.df <- data.frame(nrow(data.df))
for(i in 1: nrow(data.df))
{
adata.df[i,1]<- paste(substr(data.df[i,1],start=5,stop=7), ", ",
data.df[i,2])
}
```

```
write.table(adata.df, file = "C:/Big Data
Visualization/WebsitesByMonth.txt", sep = ",", quote = FALSE, col.names =
FALSE, row.names = FALSE)
```

When I created my new file, I instructed R to not add row and column headers and to not wrap my fields with quote characters. This will make it easier for me to process later.

The following are some sample records from my generated file:

```
Jun, http://www.readingphilles.com
Sep, http://www.hollywood.com
Sep, http://www.dice.com
Jun, http://www.farming.com
Nov, http://www.wkipedia.com
Aug, http://www.r-project.com
Oct, http://www.rpropgramming.com
Feb, http://www.aa.com
Nov, http://www.farming.com
```

Next, I created (another) simple script to count the number of websites by month.

The basic idea is that there is now, what I call, month transactions in my file (shown previously); one transaction (or record) per valid website for the month (note that there may be, and are, multiple records for each month).

So I now have effectively summarized my web log files into a count of hits for each month using the following script:

```
tmpTableSpace<-read.table("C:/Big Data Visualization/   WebsitesByMonth.txt
")
data.df <- data.frame(tmpTableSpace)
M01 <-0; M02 <-0; M03 <-0; M04 <-0; M05 <-0; M06 <-0
M07 <-0; M08 <-0; M09 <-0; M10 <-0; M11 <-0; M12 <-0
for(i in 1:nrow(data.df))
{
  if (substr(data.df[i,1],start=1,stop=3) == 'Jan') {M01 <- M01 + 1}
  if (substr(data.df[i,1],start=1,stop=3) == 'Feb') {M02 <- M02 + 1}
  if (substr(data.df[i,1],start=1,stop=3) == 'Mar') {M03 <- M03 + 1}
  if (substr(data.df[i,1],start=1,stop=3) == 'Apr') {M04 <- M04 + 1}
  if (substr(data.df[i,1],start=1,stop=3) == 'May') {M05 <- M05 + 1}
  if (substr(data.df[i,1],start=1,stop=3) == 'Jun') {M06 <- M06 + 1}
  if (substr(data.df[i,1],start=1,stop=3) == 'Jul') {M07 <- M07 + 1}
  if (substr(data.df[i,1],start=1,stop=3) == 'Aug') {M08 <- M08 + 1}
  if (substr(data.df[i,1],start=1,stop=3) == 'Sep') {M09 <- M09 + 1}
  if (substr(data.df[i,1],start=1,stop=3) == 'Oct') {M10 <- M10 + 1}
  if (substr(data.df[i,1],start=1,stop=3) == 'Nov') {M11 <- M11 + 1}
  if (substr(data.df[i,1],start=1,stop=3) == 'Dec') {M12 <- M12 + 1}
```

Now, I can visualize my data using a pie chart:

```
slices <- c(M01, M02, M03, M04, M05, M06, M07, M08, M09, M10, M11, M12)lbls
<- c("Jan", "Feb", "Mar", "Apr", "May", "Jun", "Jul", "Aug", "Sep", "Oct",
"Nov", "Dec")
pie(slices, labels = lbls, main="Pie Chart of Month Hit Counts")
```

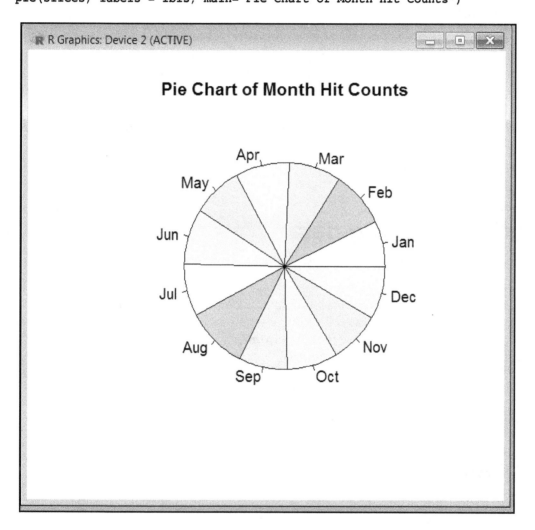

Points to consider

The preceding exercise was simply meant to make the point to the reader that not all data visualization projects require going to Hadoop (although some clearly would benefit from using Hadoop). It is obligatory for the reader to do the appropriate analysis before choosing one technology over another.

You can now see that large files can be manipulated and visualizations can be created with simple open source options such as R scripting on a machine with moderate resources. The reader must keep in mind though that such a solution may work, but may still not be appropriate as an enterprise solution. For example, processing two or three log files once or twice as part of discovery is fine, but expecting to use the process on a routine basis on files growing in number and size can quickly become a burden, inefficient, and ultimately, almost impossible.

Now, let's move onto Hadoop!

Hadoop and big data

In this section, we'll consider why Hadoop is actually a very good choice for storing and accessing big data.

Imagine you want to process data, a lot of data. In our previous example, we considered the scenario where machine generated web logging files are being produced and we want to leverage information within those files to perform some analytics and produce some (hopefully) compelling data visualizations.

Using *R* worked here, but if we extend the scenario with the idea that we will continue to receive web log files over time and the size of those files will increase, R might not be a feasible answer.

Entering Hadoop

Hadoop (as the product documentation says) is not your average database. In fact, Hadoop can store all kinds of data from many servers and websites and corporate vaults–as much as you might need or want to gather. In addition, Hadoop spreads your work across hundreds or thousands of processors and storage drives working in parallel all at the same time. Let's take a look at two practical examples using Hadoop.

AWS for Hadoop projects

If you are new to Hadoop and that is to say do not have a Hadoop environment already available, you can begin evaluating the power of Hadoop by downloading and installing one of the free Hadoop distributions. Good advice is to start any initial evaluation by running Hadoop in either local standalone or pseudo-distributed mode on a single machine. However, I strongly recommend to the reader who is new to Hadoop to not waste time downloading and configuring, but instead consider (temporally perhaps) subscribing to Hadoop as a service.

There are a variety of viable **Software as a Service (SaaS)** options of which Amazon is one of the very best. **Amazon Elastic MapReduce (EMR)** is a subscription web service that really does make it easy and cost effective to manipulate your big data projects. Amazon EMR provides a managed Hadoop framework that makes it easy, fast, and cost effective for you to distribute and process vast amounts of your data across dynamically scalable Amazon EC2 instances. Additionally, with Amazon EMR, you get a secure and reliable environment with log analysis, web indexing, data warehousing, machine learning, financial analysis, scientific simulation, and bioinformatics.

By deciding to do Hadoop on Amazon EMR, you get the benefits of the cloud:

- The ability to provision clusters of virtual servers within minutes
- You can scale the number of virtual servers in your cluster to manage your computation needs, and only pay for what you use
- Integration with other **Amazon Web Services (AWS)**
- Open source projects that run on top of the Hadoop architecture can also be run on Amazon EMR
- You can use trending business intelligence tools such as Microsoft Excel, MicroStrategy, QlikView, and Tableau with Amazon EMR to explore and visualize your data

In this book, it was easy to leverage Amazon EMR for our Hadoop use case examples.

Example 1

In our earlier scenario, we have multiple machine generated web log files. Although as we have seen that the web log files are too large to deal with MS Excel, they individually do not meet the criteria of big data. However, continuing the scenario, let's suppose we now have more than the original files as our website is perhaps generating multiple files each day. Given this presumption, we need a secure repository in which to store and then (hopefully) easily access our files.

Defining the environment

As I've mentioned, AWS provides us the ability to leverage Hadoop technology without spending all the time required to create and manage a new environment.

To use this environment, you need to first have an AWS account. Since this chapter is focused on loading and accessing big data files in a Hadoop enabled environment, we'll skip over how to create an account (to create an account, the reader can use a web browser to open: `http://aws.amazon.com`, and then click on **Create an AWS Account**).

Getting started

Getting started with our Amazon Hadoop environment is a four-step process:

1. Create a storage location (referred to as a bucket) for your data using **Amazon Simple Storage Service (S3)**.
2. Launch an Amazon cluster (this is what I call the Hadoop instance of a master and slaves). Your data is going to be stored here and this is also where Hadoop (as well as other big applications) is preloaded and ready for your use.
3. Upload your data; this is easily accomplished using Windows browse to select your file and click on upload!
4. Run (Hive) scripts (Hive is an open source, data warehouse type tool and analytic package that runs on top of Hadoop and utilizes HiveQL (its query language) that abstracts the MapReduce programming model and enables you to avoid the complexities of writing MapReduce programs in a lower-level computer language, such as Java. Yeah!).

That's really all there is to it. Let's give it a shot!

1. Open the Amazon S3 console (found at `https://console.aws.amazon.com/s3/`) and click on **Create Bucket**:

2. In the **Create a Bucket** dialog box, you can enter a bucket name, such as `bigdatavizproject`:

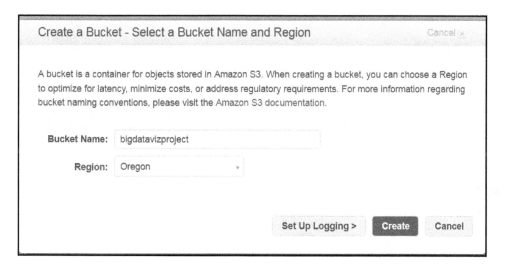

It's entirely up to you if you want to set up logging at this point.

For our exercise, you can skip that step (or not); read more about logging here:
`http://docs.aws.amazon.com/ElasticMapReduce/latest/DeveloperGuide/emr-plan-debu gging.html`).

 The bucket name should be globally unique. If the name you type is in use by another bucket, type a different name. Note that because of Hadoop requirements, Amazon S3 bucket names used with Amazon EMR must contain only lowercase letters, numbers, periods (.), and hyphens (-). Also, bucket names cannot end in numbers. For Region, choose a region for your bucket.

Once your bucket is set up, we need to create and launch a cluster. The easiest way is to click on the **cube** icon in the upper left and then click on the **EMR** icon (shown as follows):

Then, click on the **Create cluster** button (as shown in the following screenshot):

Once you click on **Create cluster**, under general configuration, enter a unique cluster name and leave all the defaults, (under software configuration, hardware configuration, and under security select all defaults) and, then click on **Create cluster** once again.

At this point, stuff is going on back at Amazon to provision your cluster based upon your selections and input. It may take several hours since they will authenticate your request by contacting you using the contact information you provided when setting up your account. During that time, if you attempt to use your cluster, you may receive messages similar to the following screenshots:

⚠ Core Instance Group: Your account is currently being verified. Verification normally takes less than 2 hours. Until your account is verified, you may not be able to launch additional instances or create additional volumes. If you are still receiving this message after more than 2 hours, please let us know by writing to aws-verification@amazon.com. We appreciate your patience..

⚠ Master Instance Group: Your account is currently being verified. Verification normally takes less than 2 hours. Until your account is verified, you may not be able to launch additional instances or create additional volumes. If you are still receiving this message after more than 2 hours, please let us know by writing to aws-verification@amazon.com. We appreciate your patience..

Once provisioned, you can proceed to create a folder structure to organize your cluster. Folder structures look very similar to folders created on your MS Windows machine using Windows Explorer.

Going back to the S3 page, you should now see your newly provisioned bucket listed under **All Buckets**. Click on the name of your bucket to see a list of folders set up in the bucket, the list will appear (at first the list will be empty).

From there, you can click on **Create Folder**:

Once you click on **Create Folder**, a new folder namespace (as shown in the following screenshot) will appear allowing you to name the new folder:

Using the same process, that you used to create the first new folder, you can add new folders until you have three new folders in your bucket:

- HiveScripts: This is where you will upload and store your Hive query files
- Input: This is where you will store data files
- Output: This is where you can write or export data to

The following screenshot shows the completed folder structure:

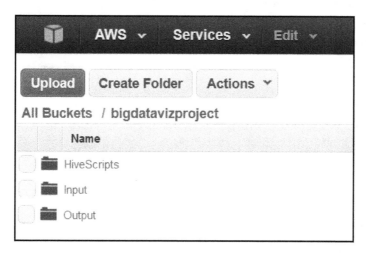

Now you are ready to start loading and processing our data files in the (Amazon) Hadoop environment. So, let's get back to our example using the multiple web log files.

Now, going back to our example, we want to upload and store our three web logging files:

```
weblog1 - 2016_08_27_01,
weblog1 - 2016_08_27_02 and
weblog1 - 2016_08_27_03:
```

The files are currently sitting in some folder on our local machine:

weblog1 -2016_08_27_01	8/27/2016 2:01 PM	Text Document	168,740 KB
weblog1 -2016_08_27_02	8/27/2016 2:01 PM	Text Document	168,740 KB
weblog1 -2016_08_27_03	8/27/2016 2:01 PM	Text Document	168,740 KB

Uploading the data

To upload our files into the Hadoop environment, you can click on the folder name (Input) within your bucket and then click on **Start Upload** (as shown in the following screenshot):

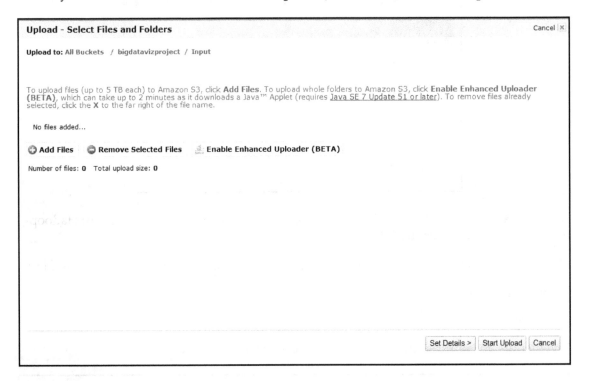

On the **Upload – Select Files and Folders** dialog (shown previously), you can click on **Add Files** and use the familiar Windows browse to locate and select each of your files.

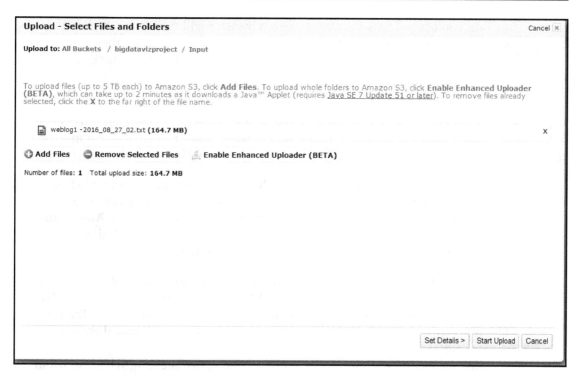

Once you select your file, click on **Start Upload** to transfer a copy of your file to your Hadoop environment bucket. The transfer progress is displayed while the file is transferring (as shown in the following screenshot):

As you upload files the status of each transfer will remain on the left of your page. Rather than continuing to clutter your page with these messages, you can check the **Automatically clear finished transfers** checkbox, which will clear the message as soon as each transfer is completed.

Although our individual web log files are not really that large, the Hadoop environment will support almost an infinite number of additional files and/or future files that may be much larger.

 In the Amazon AWS environment, the only real limit to storage space is your budget since you only pay for what you use. Administrators can use the provided **Billing & Cost Management Dashboard** to view **Month-to-Spend** amounts and particularly the **Current month-to-date balance** summary, which includes **Forecasted amount due**.

 In addition, for particularly large files, it is recommended that you leverage a web service such as AWS Snowball, which is a service intended for transferring large amounts of data. If you need to transfer less than 10 terabytes of data, Snowball might not be your most economical choice. The reader can explore Snowball at https://docs.aws.amazon.com/AWSImportExport/latest/ug/whatissnowball.html.

Once the file is uploaded, it will be displayed within your bucket's Input folder (as shown in the following screenshot):

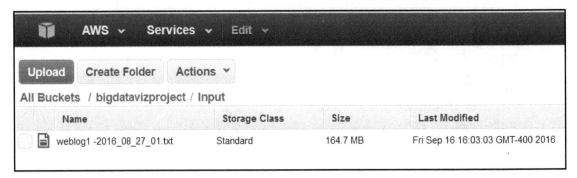

The same upload procedure that you just used to upload the first web log file can be repeated to upload the additional files (actually as many files as you want).

Manipulating the data

Once you have your data loaded into the Hadoop environment, you can start using **Hive Query Language** (**HiveQL**) provided by Amazon to manipulate the data.

Hive transparently converts your written queries to MapReduce, Apache Tez, and Spark language (saving you all that trouble), so they will seamlessly work in the Hadoop environment. In fact, if you know a bit of structured query language, you can fumble your way through Hive.

A note from the Hive documentation is as follows:

Internally, a compiler translates HiveQL statements into a directed acyclic graph of MapReduce, Apache Tez, or Spark jobs, which are submitted to Hadoop for execution. The storage and querying operations of Hive closely resemble with that of traditional databases. While Hive works on an SQL dialect, there are a lot of differences in structure and working of Hive in comparison to relational databases. The differences are mainly because Hive is built on top of the Hadoop ecosystem and has to comply with the restrictions of Hadoop and MapReduce.

Currently (at the time of writing), Hive is listed in the *Top 15 Data Management / Big Data Skills Pay* in highest demand.

> It wouldn't hurt having Hive on your resume. A comprehensive Hive language reference manual can be reviewed at:
> `https://cwiki.apache.org/confluence/display/Hive/LanguageManual`.

In our previous example, we used R programming scripts to:

1. Combine (or row-bind) multiple files into one larger file.
2. Read the combined file and create a new single file that contained only the two columns of data we were interested in.
3. Extract only the month from the first data column (which contained a string of formatted text).
4. Count the number of websites by month and create an aggregation of the data (so that it could be used to create a simple visualization).

Now that our data is in the Hadoop environment, we can use Hive scripts to accomplish the same objectives:

1. Create a single table (this will ultimately become our combined data).
2. Load our files into the single table.
3. Reformat the date column (into just month), parse out the website address.
4. Aggregate the data by month.

Notice that each approach is slightly different (for example, with R we use files while with Hive we use tables), but the end result is very much the same.

All Hive scripts can be saved as text files and uploaded to the folder you created named `HiveScripts` (using the same upload procedure used to upload your data files).

Although the file extension `.txt` works just fine, you'll probably want to organize your HiveQL files with an informative name and save them with a `.sql` extension so that they will stand out, such as `Loadweblogfiles.sql`.

A specific example

Let's look at a simple example.

The following Hive script was created and saved using MS Windows Notepad:

```
exampleone - Notepad
File  Edit  Format  View  Help

CREATE TABLE thebigdatatable (logrecord VARCHAR(550));
LOAD DATA INPATH 's3://bigdatavizproject/Input/weblog1 -2016_08_27_01.txt' INTO TABLE thebigdatatable;
select substr(ltrim(rtrim(logrecord)), 20, 3) from thebigdatatable;
```

Taking a closer look at the code, it works as follows:

```
CREATE TABLE thebigdatatable (logrecord VARCHAR(550));
LOAD DATA INPATH 's3://bigdatavizproject/Input/weblog1 -2016_08_27_01.txt'
INTO TABLE thebigdatatable;
select substr(ltrim(rtrim(logrecord)), 20, 3) from thebigdatatable;
```

- Line 1 creates a Hive table named `thebigdatatable`, which will have one column in it named `logrecord`.

- Line 2 loads all of the records in our web log file (`weblog1 -2016_08_27_01.txt`) into the table that we just created in line 1. Each record in the file becomes a single record in the table.
- Line 3 will parse the month from each record.

If we run the script, the following is a portion of the generated output showing the list of months, record by record:

```
/usr/bin/hive
Jun
Sep
Sep
Jun
Nov
Aug
Oct
Feb
Nov
Sep
Dec
Nov
Jun
Sep
Dec
Jan
Feb
May
Jan
Apr
Mar
Jan
Jun
Mar
Dec
Nov
```

Now that you know what a Hive script looks like and how to save it and upload it, we can proceed with our exercise of running more Hive scripts to duplicate what we did using *R* programming earlier in the chapter.

Although you can interactively execute Hive scripts using the **Amazon AWS Command Line Interface** (**CLI**), the easiest way (and I think the most efficient way) to run Hive scripts is by creating steps within a cluster:

1. If we go back to the main page (or the AWS console), you can click on the **EMR** icon (as shown in the following screenshot):

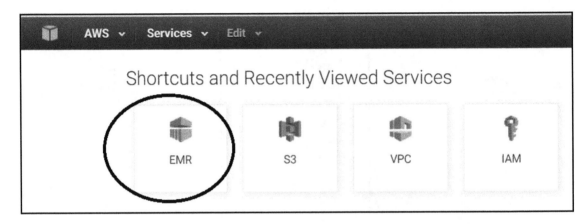

2. On the page that is displayed next, all of the clusters currently defined will be listed (as shown in the following screenshot):

3. Next, click on your cluster name (here our cluster name is `bigdatavizprojectcluster`) to open the cluster details page, as shown in the following screenshot:

4. If you scroll down the page, you will find the **Steps** section, or you can simply click on the button labeled **Add step** in the upper leftside of the page:

5. Once you click on **Add step**, the **Add Step dialog** is displayed.
6. There, select **Hive program** from the **Step** type drop-down list and then give your step a name (something more interesting than the default **Hive program**).

The name examples might be `createmonthtable` or `loadlogdata`.

Now you can use the folder icons on Windows to browse the folders you created earlier in this chapter (`HiveScripts`, `Input`, and `Output`):

- Select the Hive script file from the `HiveSripts` folder
- Select the `Input` folder (where our web log files have been loaded)
- Select the `Output` folder as the **Output S3 location**

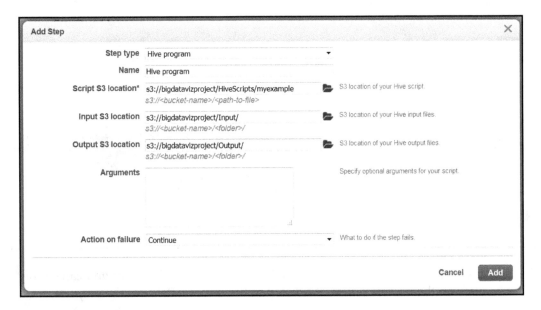

When you have provided the preceding details, click on **Add** in the lower-right corner of the dialog.

This will submit your cluster step to be run in batch mode within your cluster.

The progress of your step will be displayed in the steps section of the cluster details page.

Consider the following screenshot as an example:

Now, let's go ahead and write and run a few more interesting Hive scripts.

Once we've created our table named `thebigdatatable` (shown earlier), we can use another Hive script to load each of our files into the table using the same HiveQL command (OAD DATA):

```
LOAD DATA INPATH 's3://bigdatavizproject/Input/weblog1 -2016_08_27_01.txt'
INTO TABLE thebigdatatable;
LOAD DATA INPATH 's3://bigdatavizproject/Input/weblog1 -2016_08_27_02.txt'
INTO TABLE thebigdatatable;
LOAD DATA INPATH 's3://bigdatavizproject/Input/weblog1 -2016_08_27_03.txt'
INTO TABLE thebigdatatable;
```

This will load all of the records from all of the files into the same single table.

Notice that the command simply indicates LOAD DATA with an explicit file location and name reference as well as INTO TABLE also with an explicit name of a table to be loaded with the data.

Therefore, we have now created our one big single file (like we did using *R*). Another key point is, we've loaded somewhat unstructured web log data into a structured database table.

Moving on, we can use the following Hive script to create two formatted columns (out of each table record):

```
select substr(substr(logrecord, instr(logrecord,'['), 12),5,3),
substr(logrecord, instr(logrecord,'www'), 250) from thebigdatatable;
```

This script utilizes the `substr` and `instr` HiveQL functions to parse the month name and website address from the record.

Here is the pending Hive step shown that will execute the preceding script:

The following is a portion of the output generated upon completion of the script, showing the two columns, the month and the website address:

```
/usr/bin/hive
Jun        www.readingphilles.com
Sep        www.hollywood.com
Sep        www.dice.com
Jun        www.farming.com
Nov        www.wkipedia.com
Aug        www.r-project.com
Oct        www.rpropgramming.com
Feb        www.aa.com
Nov        www.farming.com
Sep        www.perl.com
Dec        www.quail.com
Nov        www.cognos.com
Jun        www.GQ.com
Sep        www.dragracing.com
Dec        www.gazette.com
Jan        www.delta.com
Feb        www.wkipedia.com
May        www.phillies.com
Jan        www.coursera.com
Apr        www.coursera.com
Mar        www.movies.com
Jan        www.libraryedu.com
Jun        www.farming.com
Mar        www.usair.com
Dec        www.cosmos.com
```

Next, the following script can be used to create a new formatted column table using a subquery as input (which we will then be able to use to perform the aggregate of data and calculate our month counts).

The columns of this new table (named `dabigdatatable`) will be `mydate` and `mysite`:

```
CREATE TABLE dabigdatatable (mydate VARCHAR(64), mysite VARCHAR(64));
```

Next, we can use the following script to load our new table with our formatted records:

```
insert overwrite table dabigdatatable
select substr (substr (logrecord, instr(logrecord,'['), 12),5,3),
substr(logrecord, instr(logrecord,'www'), 250) from thebigdatatable;
```

And, finally, the following script will list the total count values by month:

```
select mydate, count(distinct(mysite)) from dabigdatatable group by mydate
```

The following is the partial output generated from the previous script:

```
/usr/bin/hive
Apr        59
Aug        59
Dec        59
Feb        59
Jan        59
Jul        59
Jun        59
Mar        59
May        59
Nov        59
Oct        59
Sep        59
```

Conclusion

In the Hadoop exercise of this chapter, we have pretty much accomplished all of the tasks we originally completed using *R* programming. Although the actual HiveQL query statements may not be written in the most optimal way, (there are many ways to accomplish the same thing with HiveQL, for example, one could submit all of the queries in one HiveQL batch file and as a single cluster step) a few of the advantages of using Hadoop are:

- You have more space to easily store more (and larger) files
- Using Hive, you can easily manipulate the data in bulk using the Hive QL
- The AWS Hadoop environment allowed us to run the Hive scripts in a much shorter time than it took for us to run our R scripts
- You can submit your scripts in batch mode, which is more efficient than running interactive commands when processing larger files
- We easily loaded and manipulated somewhat unstructured data

Example 2

Let's consider a few more examples.

As already mentioned, the HiveQL language is very similar to standard SQL, and it's worthy of the time taken to explore some additional data manipulations using HiveQL.

A key point is that while Hive is intended as a convenience/interface for querying large amounts of data stored in HDFS, SQL is more intended for online operations requiring many reads and writes, which is very similar with somewhat different objectives.

The following script can be used to identify the unique websites viewed in a particular month (the month of June) using the DISTINCT HiveQL function:

```
select distinct(mysite) from dabigdatatable where mydate = 'Jun'
```

This would yield the following (partial) output:

```
/usr/bin/hive
www.GQ.com
www.aa.com
www.amazon.com
www.anaplan.com
www.apple.com
www.appstore.com
www.bioinformatic
www.cnn.com
www.cognos.com
www.colts.com
www.cosmos.com
www.coursera.com
www.delta.com
www.dice.com
www.dragracing.co
www.eagles.com
www.farming.com
www.feetfirst.com
www.forbes.com
www.gazette.com
www.hilory.com
www.hollywood.com
www.hotels.com
www.hp.com
www.ironpigs.com
www.libraryedu.co
www.lookup.com
www.magabus.com
www.microsoft.com
www.miller.com
www.monster.com
www.movies.com
www.msn.com
www.napa.com
www.nasa.com
```

Sorting

Just like with standard query language, you can sort (or reorder) your output (of unique websites) using a script similar to the following:

```
select distinct(mysite) from dabigdatatable where mydate = 'Jun' order by
mysite
```

This HiveQL script creates an ordered list of the website addresses visited in the month of June.

The following output is generated and (partially) displayed as shown:

```
/usr/bin/hive
www.GQ.com
www.aa.com
www.amazon.com
www.anaplan.com
www.apple.com
www.appstore.com
www.bioinformatics.com
www.cnn.com
www.cognos.com
www.colts.com
www.cosmos.com
www.coursera.com
www.delta.com
www.dice.com
www.dragracing.com
www.eagles.com
www.farming.com
www.feetfirst.com
www.forbes.com
www.gazette.com
www.hilory.com
www.hollywood.com
www.hotels.com
www.hp.com
www.ironpigs.com
www.libraryedu.com
www.lookup.com
www.magabus.com
www.microsoft.com
```

You might notice that the first website address (www.GQ.com) doesn't seem like it's ordered within the list correctly. This is because of case-sensitivity. A simple modification to the HiveQL (adding the ucase function) might make more sense:

```
select distinct(mysite) from dabigdatatable where mydate = 'Jun' order by
ucase(mysite)
```

Running this modified HiveQL script now generates the following output (partially displayed as shown):

```
/usr/bin/hive
www.aa.com
www.amazon.com
www.anaplan.com
www.apple.com
www.appstore.com
www.bioinformatics.com
www.cnn.com
www.cognos.com
www.colts.com
www.cosmos.com
www.coursera.com
www.delta.com
www.dice.com
www.dragracing.com
www.eagles.com
www.farming.com
www.feetfirst.com
www.forbes.com
www.gazette.com
www.GQ.com
www.hilory.com
www.hollywood.com
www.hotels.com
www.hp.com
www.ironpigs.com
www.libraryedu.com
www.lookup.com
www.magabus.com
www.microsoft.com
```

Earlier in this chapter, we created the table named `thebigdatatable`. We then used this table to load our individual files and combine them into one large data source (one single table). Later, we used HiveQL scripts to do some aggregations to count the number of distinct website addresses for each month.

This time, let's go back and look at individual IP addresses found in the log files.

Parsing the IP

The IP addresses can be parsed from the log records with the `instr` and `substr` functions, similar to how we found the month name and the web addresses:

```
count(substr(logrecord, 1, (instr(logrecord,'-')-2)))
```

The month can be again found within the record using the same functions:

```
substr(substr(logrecord, instr(logrecord,'['), 12),5,3)
```

Earlier we used HiveQL to create and load a formatted column table, which we then ran aggregation scripts against. This time, let's do it in a single HiveQL script (not bothering with creating a new table).

The following script can be used:

```
select substr(substr(logrecord, instr(logrecord,'['), 12),5,3),
count(substr(logrecord, 1, (instr(logrecord,'-')-2)))
from thebigdatatable group by substr(substr(logrecord,
instr(logrecord,'['), 12),5,3);
```

This gives us the desired output (as shown in the following screenshot):

```
/usr/bin/hive
Apr        90984
Aug        102551
Dec        87445
Feb        92368
Jan        74878
Jul        86173
Jun        91826
Mar        88219
May        83731
Nov        84281
Oct        85283
Sep        80837
```

Although the actual number counts of the IP addresses for each month are quite large, the preceding output can be visualized as a simple bar chart using the `barplot` R function:

```
counts <-
c(74878,92368,88219,90984,83731,91826,86173,102551,80837,85283,84281,87445)
barplot(counts, main="IP Counts By Month",
    xlab="Number of Distinct IPs")
```

This produces the following graph:

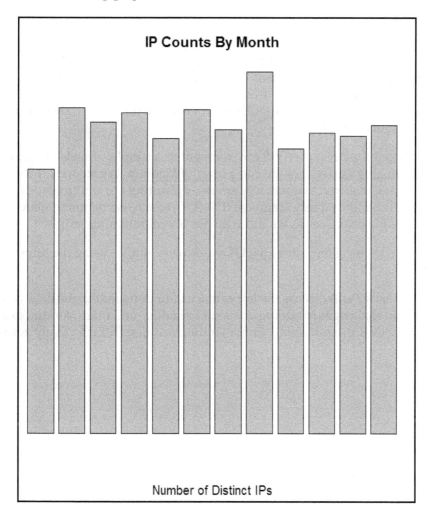

Although, in this chapter, we have just scratched the surface of the power and features (which are still growing) of using Amazon AWS, the reader should be able to see its potential for big data projects and is encouraged to continue to explore its capabilities.

One excellent source I found is the *Amazon Big Data Blog*, whose moniker is *Helping you collect, store, clean, process, and visualize big data,* and it can be reviewed at `http://blogs.aws.amazon.com/bigdata`.

Summary

In this chapter, we provided the reader with a high-level definition of Hadoop, including some fun Hadoop FAQs. We mentioned that simply reaching MS Excel limitations doesn't mean that you are actually dealing with big data and used simple examples of R programming scripts to actually manipulate and visualize that same data that would not load in Excel to prove that point.

We then introduced the Amazon AWS environment as a simple, affordable, yet robust solution for leveraging the technology and power of Hadoop. We stepped through the process configuring that environment for our use, uploading our multiple web log files to it, and then used Hive and its query language (HiveQL) to access and manipulate that data to accomplish the same objectives as we did with our R programming scripts.

Finally, we offered some alternative HiveQL working examples using the same uploaded web log data.

In the next chapter, we will discuss the importance of understanding the data you are working with, the challenges of adding context to big data, and offer working examples using more complex R programming demonstrating solutions for effectively addressing these issues.

3
Understanding Your Data Using R

In this chapter, we will explore the idea of adding context to the data you are working with.

Specifically, we'll discuss the importance of establishing data context, as well as the practice of profiling your data for context discovery and how big data affects this effort.

At some point, you will perhaps discover that although the big data sources you have access to have the potential to positively impact your marketing efforts, profitability, decision making, or even your life, there also exists the risk of drawing incorrect conclusions from that same data. In fact, one could argue that the bigger the data, the bigger the risk. Thankfully, by properly profiling your data, you can see the big picture that your data provides a bit more clearly (that is, putting your data in context).

This chapter is organized into the following main sections:

- Adding context
- About R
- R and big data
- Example 1
- Example 2

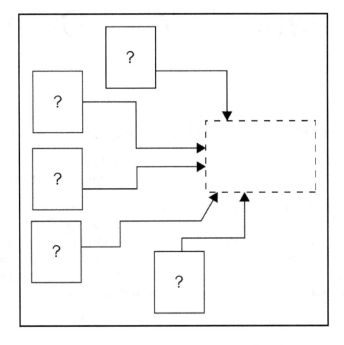

In Chapter 2, *Access, Speed, and Storage with Hadoop,* we explored a scenario where multiple (web logging) files were loaded into a Hadoop environment where they could be accessed and queried as a single data source or a single file.

In that example, all of our files came from the same source (and were in the same format). Realistically, those individual data files may be sourced from a variety of places which, potentially, could influence the data's potential meaning or value.

Generally speaking, similar-looking data can actually mean very different things. For example, an average heart rate carries a significantly different connotation if the median age of patients within a pool or group of data is 18-25 versus the same average for patients older than 65.

When writing a book, authors leave context clues for their readers. A context clue is a source of information that helps readers understand written content that may be difficult or unique. This information offers insight into the content being read or consumed (an example might be, "It was an idyllic day: sunny, warm, and perfect...").

With data, context clues should be developed through a process referred to as profiling (we'll discuss profiling in more detail later in this chapter) so that the data consumer can better understand the data when visualized. Additionally, having context and perspective on the data you are working with is a vital step in determining what kind of data visualization should be created.

Context or profiling examples might be calculating the average age of patients or subjects within the data or segmenting the data into time periods (years or months, usually).

Another motive for adding context to data might be to gain a new perspective on the data. An example of this might be recognizing and examining a comparison present in the data. For example, body fat percentages of urban high school seniors could be compared to those of rural high school seniors.

Adding context to your data before creating visualizations can certainly make it (the data visualization) more relevant, but context still can't serve as a substitute for value. Before you consider any factors such as time of day, or geographic location, or average age, first and foremost, your data visualization needs to benefit those who are going to consume it, so establishing appropriate context requirements will be critical.

 For data profiling (adding context), the rule is: before context, think of a value.

Generally speaking, there are several contextual visualization categories, which can be used to augment or increase the value and understanding of data for visualization.

These include the following:

- Definitions and explanations
- Comparisons
- Contrasts
- Tendencies
- Dispersion

Definitions and explanations

This is providing additional information or attributes about a data point.

Patient ID	Height	Weight	BMI
10000001	6.2	195	22.60727
10000002	5.9	200	23.76913
10000003	6.0	180	21.2132
10000004	5.1	145	18.51684

Comparisons

This is adding a comparable value to a particular data point. For example, you might compute and add a national ranking to each total by state:

State	Cancer Patients	Cancer Patients v National Average
NJ	22	23
PA	21	24
CA	23	29

Contrasts

This is almost like adding an opposite to a data point to see if it perhaps determines a different perspective. An example might be reviewing average body weights for patients who consume alcoholic beverages versus those who do not consume alcoholic beverages:

Avg. Body Weight (Alcohol)	Avg. Body Weight (No Alcohol)
189.0	165.0

Tendencies

These are the typical mathematical calculations (or summaries) on the data as a whole or by other categories within the data, such as mean, median, and mode. For example, you might add a **Median Heart Rate for Age Group** that each patient in the data is a member of:

Patient ID	Average Heart Rate	Median Heart Rate for Age Group
10000001	66	71
10000002	100	71
10000003	73	71
10000004	90	71

Dispersion

Again, these are mathematical calculations (or summaries), such as range, variance, and standard deviation, but they describe the average of a dataset (or group within the data). For example, you may want to add the range to a selected value, such as the minimum and a maximum number of hospital stays found in the data for each patient age group:

Patient ID	No Hospital Stays	Hospital Stays Range by age group
10000001	0	0-5
10000002	3	0-5
10000003	2	0-9
10000004	5	0-6

The art of profiling data to add context and identify new and interesting perspectives for visualization is still and ever evolving; no doubt there are additional contextual categories existing today that can be investigated as you continue your work with big data visualization projects.

Adding context

So, how do we add context to data? Is it merely select **Insert**, then **Data Context**?

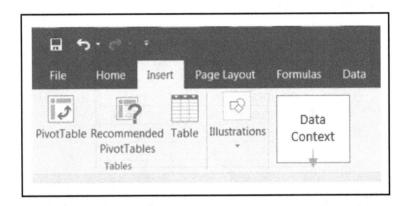

No, it's not that easy (but it's not impossible either).

Once you have identified (or pulled together) your big data source (or at least a significant amount of data), how do you go from mountains of raw big data to summarizations that can be used as input to create valuable data visualizations, helping you to further analyze that data and support your conclusions?

The answer is through data profiling.

Data profiling involves logically getting to know the data you think you may want to visualize through query, experimentation, and review.

Following the profiling process, you can then use the information you have collected to add context (and/or apply new perspectives) to the data. Adding context to data requires the manipulation of data to perhaps reformat, adding calculations, aggregations, or additional columns or re-ordering, and so on.

Finally, you will be ready to visualize (or picture) your data.

The complete profiling process is as follows:

1. **Pull together** the data or enough of the data.
2. **Profile** the data through query, experimentation, and review.

2. Add **Perspective**(s) or context.
3. **Picture** (visualize) the data.

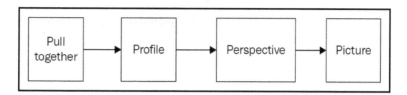

About R

We've dabbled a little bit in `Chapter 2`, *Access, Speed, and Storage with Hadoop*, with R programming, but in this chapter, we now formally introduce R as the tool to perform our data profiling exercises as well as adding perspectives (establish context) for data to be used in visualizations.

R is a language and environment easy to learn, very flexible in nature, and also very focused on statistical computing thus making it great for manipulating, cleaning, summarizing, producing probability statistics, and so on (as well as actually creating visualizations with your data), so it's a great choice for the exercises required for profiling, establishing context, and identifying additional perspectives.

In addition, here are a few more reasons to use R when profiling your big data:

- R is used by a large number of academic statisticians, so it's a tool that is not going away.
- R is pretty much platform independent, what you develop will run almost anywhere.
- R has awesome help resources–just Google it; you'll see!

R and big data

Although R is free (open sourced), super flexible, and feature rich, you must keep in mind that R preserves everything in your machine's memory and this can become problematic when you are working with big data (even with the introduction of the low resource costs of today).

Thankfully, though, there are various options and strategies to work with this limitation, such as imploring a sort of pseudo-sampling technique, which we will expound on later in this chapter (as part of some of the examples provided).

Additionally, R libraries have been developed and introduced that can leverage hard drive space (as sort of a virtual extension of your machine's memory), again exposed in this chapter's examples.

Example 1

In this chapter's first example, we'll use data collected from a theoretical hospital where upon admission, information about a patient's medical history is collected through an online survey. Information is also added to a patient's file as treatment is provided.

The file includes many fields, including basic descriptive data for the patient, such as:

- sex
- DOBMonth, DOBDay, DOBYear
- height
- weight
- Bloodtype

Vital statistics, such as:

- blood_pressure
- heartrate

Medical history, such as:

- no_hospital_visits
- Surgeries
- Major illnesses or conditions
- Whether currently under a doctor's care

Demographical statistics, such as:

- Occupation
- Home state
- Educational background

Some additional information is also collected in the file in an attempt to develop patient characters and habits such as the number of times the patient included beef, pork, and fowl in their weekly diet, or whether they typically use a butter replacement product, and so on.

Periodically, the data is dumped to text files, are comma-delimited, and contain the following fields (in this order):

```
Patientid, recorddate_month, recorddate_day, recorddate_year, sex, age,
weight, height, no_hospital_visits, heartrate, state, relationship,
Insured, Bloodtype, blood_pressure, Education, DOBMonth, DOBDay, DOBYear,
current_smoker,
current_drinker, currently_on_medications, known_allergies,
currently_under_doctors_care, ever_operated_on, occupation, Heart_attack,
Rheumatic_Fever   Heart_murmur, Diseases_of_the_arteries, Varicose_veins,
Arthritis, abnormal_bloodsugar, Phlebitis, Dizziness_fainting,
Epilepsy_seizures, Stroke, Diphtheria, Scarlet_Fever,
Infectious_mononucleosis, Nervous_emotional_problems, Anemia,
hyroid_problems, Pneumonia, Bronchitis, Asthma, Abnormal_chest_Xray,
lung_disease, Injuries_back_arms_legs_joints_Broken_bones,
Jaundice_gallbladder_problems, Father_alive, Father_current_age,
Fathers_general_health, Fathers_reason_poor_health,
Fathersdeceased_age_death, mother_alive, Mother_current_age,
Mother_general_health, Mothers_reason_poor_health,
Mothers_deceased_age_death, No_of_brothers, No_of_sisters,
age_range, siblings_health_problems, Heart_attacks_under_50,
Strokes_under_50, High_blood_pressure, Elevated_cholesterol,
Diabetes, Asthma_hayfever, Congenital_heart_disease,
Heart_operations, Glaucoma, ever_smoked_cigs, cigars_or_pipes,
no_cigs_day, no_cigars_day, no_pipefuls_day,
if_stopped_smoking_when_was_it,
if_still_smoke_how_long_ago_start,target_weight,
most_ever_weighed, 1_year_ago_weight, age_21_weight,
No_of_meals_eatten_per_day, No_of_times_per_week_eat_beef,
No_of_times_per_week_eat_pork, No_of_times_per_week_eat_fish,
No_of_times_per_week_eat_fowl, No_of_times_per_week_eat_desserts,
No_of_times_per_week_eat_fried_foods,
No_servings_per_week_wholemilk,
No_servings_per_week_2%_milk,
No_servings_per_week_tea,
No_servings_per_week_buttermilk,
No_servings_per_week_1%_milk,
No_servings_per_week_regular_or_diet_soda,
No_servings_per_week_skim_milk, No_servings_per_week_coffee
No_servings_per_week_water, beer_intake, wine_intake, liquor_intake,
use_butter, use_extra_sugar, use_extra_salt,
different_diet_weekends, activity_level, sexually_active,
vision_problems, wear_glasses
```

The following is a screenshot showing a portion of the file (displayed in MS Windows Notepad):

```
sampleHCSurvey01 - Notepad                                          _  □  X

File  Edit  Format  View  Help
000001,Aug/16/2010,Male,66,70,160,5,150,Rhode Island,Divorced,Yes,O-positive,134/87,Other a
000002,Jun/20/2000,Male,57,70,160,6,160,Nebraska,Single,No,AB-positive,131/86,Masters degre
000003,Jun/16/2011,Female,75,65,130,0,150,Nevada,Divorced,No,A-negative,134/87,Masters degr
000004,May/3/2012,Female,88,65,130,6,150,Florida,Married,No,B-positive,134/87,Completed son
000005,Jun/2/2014,Female,84,65,130,10,150,South Carolina,Other,No,A-positive,134/87,Bachelc
000006,Mar/18/2010,Male,59,70,160,2,160,Indiana,Single,No,O-positive,131/86,Other advanced
000007,Mar/19/2010,Male,25,70,160,9,190,Illinois,Married,No,AB-positive,121/80,Masters degr
000008,Apr/24/2007,Female,86,65,130,6,150,Missouri,Married,Yes,O-negative,134/87,High schoc
000009,Jun/28/2016,Female, 8,50,58,2,200,Louisiana,Divorced,No,B-positive,122/78,Completed
000010,Dec/29/2010,Male,79,70,160,5,150,Texas,Married,No,O-negative,134/87,Associate degree
```

Assuming we have been given no further information about the data, other than the provided field name list and the knowledge that the data is captured by hospital personnel upon patient admission, the next step would be to perform some sort of profiling of the data investigating to start understanding the data and then to start adding context and perspectives (so ultimately we can create some visualizations).

Initially, we start out by looking through the field or column names in our file and some ideas start to come to mind. For example, what is the data time frame we are dealing with? Using the field record date, can we establish a period of time (or time frame) for the data? (In other words, over what period of time was this data captured).

Can we start grouping the data using fields such as `sex`, `age`, and `state`?

Eventually, what we should be asking is, what can we learn from visualizing the data? Perhaps:

- What is the breakdown of those currently smoking by `age` group?
- What is the ratio of those currently smoking to the number of hospital visits?
- Do the patients currently under a doctor's care, on an average, have better BMI ratios?

Digging in with R

Using the power of R programming, we can run various queries on the data; noting that the results of these queries may spawn additional questions and queries and eventually, yield data ready for visualizing.

Let's start with a few simple profile queries. I always start my data profiling by time boxing the data.

The following R scripts (although as mentioned earlier, there are many ways to accomplish the same objective) work well for this:

```
# --- read our file into a temporary R table
tmpRTable4TimeBox<-read.table(file="C:/Big Data Visualization/Chapter
3/sampleHCSurvey02.txt", sep=",")

# --- convert to an R data frame and filter it to just include # --- the
2nd column or field of data
data.df <- data.frame(tmpRTable4TimeBox)
data.df <- data.df[,2]

# --- provides a sorted list of the years in the file
YearsInData = substr(substr(data.df[], (regexpr('/',data.df[])+1),11),(
regexpr('/',substr(data.df[], (regexpr('/',data.df[])+1),11))+1),11)
# -- write a new file named ListofYears
write.csv(sort(unique(YearsInData)),file="C:/Big Data Visualization
/Chapter 3/ListofYears.txt",quote = FALSE, row.names = FALSE)
```

The preceding simple R script provides a sorted list file (`ListofYears.txt` shown in the following screenshot) containing the years found in the data we are profiling:

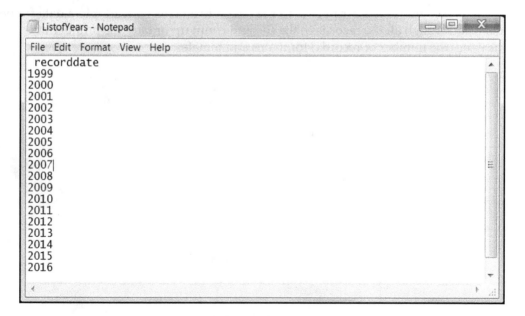

Now we can see that our patient survey data covers patient survey data collected during the years 1999 through 2016 and with this information we start to add context (or allow us to gain a perspective) on our data.

We could further time-box the data by perhaps breaking the years into months (we will do this later on in this chapter), but let's move on now to some basic grouping profiling.

Assuming that each record in our data represents a unique hospital visit, how can we determine the number of hospital visits (the number of records) by sex, age, and state?

Here I will point out that it may be worthwhile establishing the size (number of rows or records (we already know the number of columns or fields) of the file you are working with. This is important since the size of the data file will dictate the programming or scripting approach that you will need to use during your profiling.

Simple R functions that are valuable to know are nrow and head. These simple commands can be used to count the total rows in a file:

```
nrow:mydata
```

To view the first *n* number of rows of data, use the following code:

```
head(mydata, nrow=10)
```

So, using R, one could write a script to load the data into a table, convert it to a data frame, and then read through all the records in the file and count up or tally the number of hospital visits (the number of records) for males and females.

Such logic is a snap to write:

```
# --- assuming tmpRTable holds the data already
datas.df<-data.frame(tmpRTable)

# --- initialize 2 counter variables
NumberMaleVisits <-0;NumberFemaleVisits <-0

# --- read through the data
for(i in 1:nrow(datas.df))
{
  if (datas.df[i,3] == 'Male')
  {
    NumberMaleVisits <- NumberMaleVisits + 1
  }
  if (datas.df[i,3] == 'Female')
  {
    NumberFemaleVisits <- NumberFemaleVisits + 1
  }
```

```
}

# --- show me the totals
NumberMaleVisits
NumberFemaleVisits
```

The preceding script works, but in a big data scenario, there is a more efficient way, since reading or looping through and counting each record will take far too long. Thankfully, R provides the table function, which can be used similar to the SQL group by command.

The following script assumes that our data is already in an R data frame (named datas.df), so using the sequence number of the field in the file, if we want to see the number of hospital visits for males and the number of hospital visits for females, we can write the following:

```
# --- using R table function as "group by" field number
# --- patient sex is the 3rd field in the file

table(datas.df[,3])
```

The following is the output generated from running the preceding script. Notice that R shows sex with a count of 1 since the script included the files header record of the file as a unique value:

```
> table(datas.df[,3])

  sex Female    Male
    1  65661   60581
>
```

We can also establish the number of hospital visits by `state` (`state` is the ninth field in the file):

```
table(datas.df[,9])
```

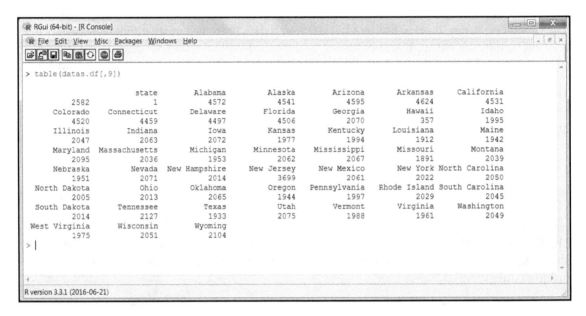

Age (or the fourth field in the file) can also be studied using the R functions `Sort` and `table`:

```
sort(table(datas.df[,4]))
```

 Since there are quite a few more values for age within the file, I've sorted the output using the R `sort` function:

```
> sort(table(datas.df[,4]))

  age   35   43   61    1   25    4   68    9   93   16   23   12   50   17   10   29   94   58   55   45   88   78
    1 1167 1193 1198 1203 1212 1214 1217 1219 1219 1220 1220 1225 1228 1229 1234 1234 1234 1238 1240 1242 1242 1243
   33    8   19   80   98   49   62   30   57   34   31   67   91   92   54   77    3   47   28   71   22   72   32
 1244 1245 1245 1246 1248 1249 1251 1252 1252 1255 1257 1258 1260 1260 1261 1261 1262 1263 1264 1264 1267 1267 1273
   82   83   37   73   74   63   66    2   76   11   27   52   20   36   42    7   13   48   69   44   56   99    5
 1273 1276 1277 1277 1278 1279 1281 1282 1283 1284 1284 1285 1286 1286 1286 1288 1290 1290 1290 1293 1293 1293 1294
   84   81   86   65   75   60   64   97   24   87   46   79   90   51   89   14   59   96   38   39   15   18   21
 1294 1298 1298 1302 1302 1305 1306 1306 1307 1308 1310 1310 1311 1312 1312 1314 1315 1315 1317 1320 1321 1331 1333
   53    6   85   26   95   41   70   40
 1334 1336 1336 1339 1340 1348 1361 1378
> |
```

Moving on now, let's see if there is a difference between the number of hospital visits for patients who are current smokers (field name `current_smoker` and is field number 16 in the file) and those indicating that they are noncurrent smokers.

We can use the same R scripting logic:

```
sort(table(datas.df[16]))
```

Surprisingly, (one might think) it appears from our profiling that those patients who currently do not smoke have had more hospital visits (113,681) than those who currently are smokers (12,561):

```
> sort(table(datas.df[16]))

current_smoker          Yes           No
             1        12561       113681
> |
```

Another interesting R script to continue profiling our data might be:

```
table(datas.df[,3],datas.df[,16])
```

The preceding script again uses the R `table` function to group data, but shows how we can group within a group, in other words, using this script we can get totals for current and noncurrent smokers, grouped by `sex`.

In the following screenshot, we see that the difference between female smokers and male smokers might be considered to be marginal:

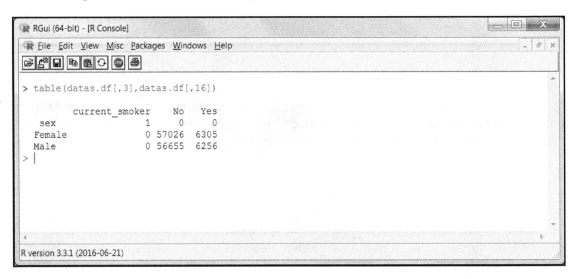

So we see that using the preceding simple R script examples, we've been able to add some context to our healthcare survey data. By reviewing the list of fields provided in the file, we can come up with the R profiling queries shown (and many others) without much effort. We will continue with some more complex profiling in the next section, but for now, let's use R to create a few data visualizations based upon what we've learned so far through our profiling.

Going back to the number of hospital visits by `sex`, we can use the R function `barplot` to create a visualization of visits by `sex`. But first, let's look at a couple of helpful hints for creating the script.

First, rather than using the table function, you can use the `ftable` function, which creates a flat version of the original function's output. This makes it easier to exclude the header record count of one that comes back from the table function.

Next, we can leverage some additional arguments of the barplot function, such as `col`, `border`, `names.arg`, and `title` to make the visualization a little nicer to look at.

The following is the script:

```
# -- use ftable function to drop out the header record
forChart<- ftable(datas.df[,3])
# --- create bar names
barnames<-c("Female","Male")
# -- use barplot to draw bar visual
barplot(forChart[2:3], col = "brown1", border = TRUE, names.arg = barnames)

# --- add a title
title(main = list("Hospital Visits by Sex", font = 4))
```

The script's output (our visualization) is as follows:

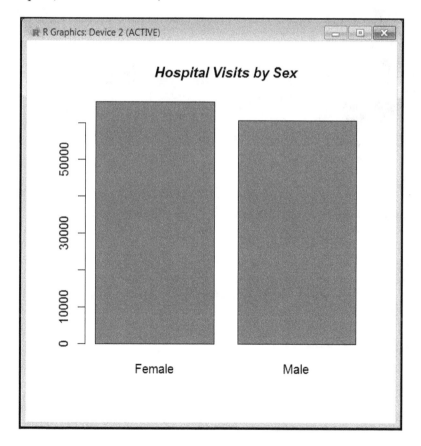

We could follow the same logic for creating a similar visualization of hospital visits by state:

```
st<-ftable(datas.df[,9])
barplot(st)
title(main = list("Hospital Visits by State", font = 2))
```

But the visualization generated isn't very clear:

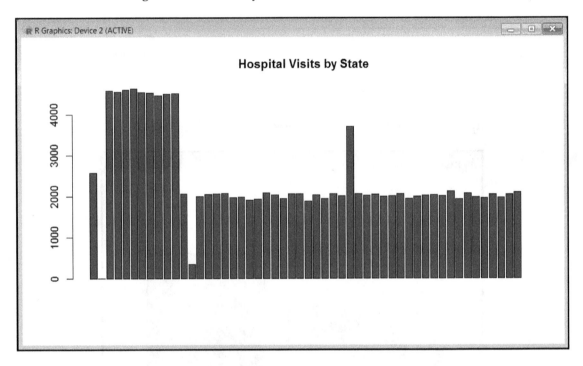

One can always experiment a bit more with this data to make the visualization a little more interesting. Using the R functions `substr` and `regexpr`, we can create an R data frame that contains a record for each `Hospital Visits by State` within each year in the file. Then we can use the function plot (rather than the `barplot` function) to generate the visualization.

The following is the R script:

```
# --- create a data frame from our original table file
datas.df <- data.frame(tmpRTable)

# --- create a filtered data frame of records from the file
# --- using the record year and state fields from the file
dats.df<-
data.frame(substr(substr(datas.df[,2],(regexpr('/',datas.df[,2])+1),11),(
```

```
regexpr('/',substr(datas.df[,2],(regexpr('/',datas.df[,2])+1),11))+1),11),d
atas.df[,9])

# --- plot to show a visualization
plot(sort(table(dats.df[2]),decreasing = TRUE),type="o", col="blue")
title(main = list("Hospital Visits by State (Highest to Lowest)", font =
2))
```

Here is the different (perhaps more interesting) version of the visualization generated by the preceding script:

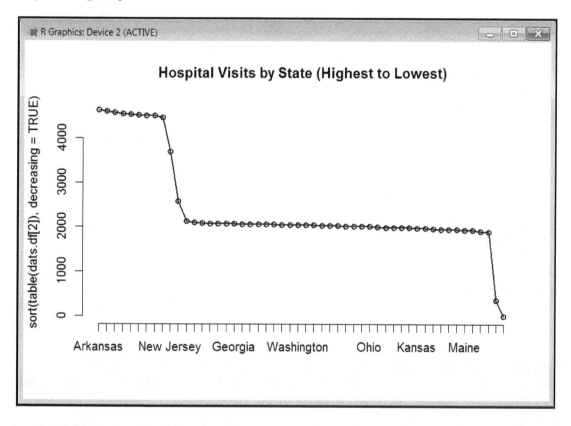

Another earlier perspective on the data was concerning Age. We grouped the hospital visits by the age of the patients (using the R table function). Since there are many different patient ages, a common practice is to establish age ranges, such as the following:

- 21 and under
- 22 to 34
- 35 to 44

- 45 to 54
- 55 to 64
- 65 and over

To implement the preceding age ranges, we need to organize the data and could use the following R script:

```
# --- initialize age range counters
a1 <-0;a2 <-0;a3 <-0;a4 <-0;a5 <-0;a6 <-0

# --- read and count visits by age range
for(i in 2:nrow(datas.df))
{
  if (as.numeric(datas.df[i,4]) < 22) {a1 <- a1 + 1}
  if (as.numeric(datas.df[i,4]) > 21 & as.numeric(datas.df[i,4]) < 35)
  {
    a2 <- a2 + 1
  }
  if (as.numeric(datas.df[i,4]) > 34 & as.numeric(datas.df[i,4]) < 45)
  {
    a3 <- a3 + 1
  }
  if (as.numeric(datas.df[i,4]) > 44 & as.numeric(datas.df[i,4]) <
  55)
  {
    a4 <- a4 + 1
  }
  if (as.numeric(datas.df[i,4]) > 54 & as.numeric(datas.df[i,4]) < 65)
  {
    a5 <- a5 + 1
  }
  if (as.numeric(datas.df[i,4]) > 64) {a6 <- a6 + 1}
}
```

Looping or reading through each of the records in our file isn't very practical if there are a trillion records. Later in this chapter, we'll use a much better approach, but for now we will assume a smaller file size for convenience.

Once the preceding script is run, we can use the R pie function and the following code to create our pie chart visualization:

```
# --- create Pie Chart

slices <- c(a1, a2, a3, a4, a5, a6)
lbls <- c("under 21", "22-34","35-44","45-54","55-64", "65 & over")
pie(slices, labels = lbls, main="Hospital Visits by Age Range")
```

The following is the generated visualization:

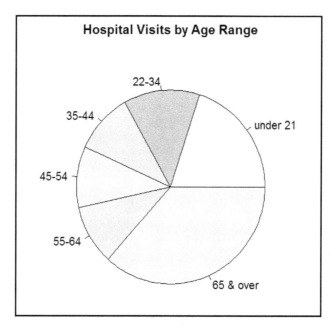

Finally, earlier in this section, we looked at the values in field 16 of our file–which indicates whether the survey patient was a current smoker. We could build a simple visual showing the totals, but (again) the visualization isn't very interesting or all that informative.

With some simple R scripts, we can proceed to create a visualization showing the number of hospital visits, year-over-year by those patients that are current smokers.

First, we can reformat the data in our R data frame (named `datas.df`) to store only the year (of the record date) using the R function `substr`. This makes it a little easier to aggregate the data by year shown in the next steps.

The R script using the `substr` function is as follows:

```
# --- redefine the record date field to hold just the record
# --- year value
datas.df[,2]<-
substr(substr(datas.df[,2],(regexpr('/',datas.df[,2])+1),11),(
regexpr('/',substr(datas.df[,2],(regexpr('/',datas.df[,2])+1),11))+1),11)
```

Next, we can create an R `table` named `c` to hold the record date year and totals (of non and current smokers) for each year.

The following is the R script that is used:

```
# --- create a table holding record year and total count for
# --- smokers and not smoking
c<-table(datas.df[,2],datas.df[,16])
```

Finally, we can use the R `barplot` function to create our visualization.

Again, there is more than likely a cleverer way to set up the objects `bars` and `lbls`, but for now, I simply handcoded the year's data I wanted to see in my visualization:

```
# --- set up the values to chart and the labels for each bar
# --- in the chart
bars<-c(c[2,3], c[3,3],
c[4,3],c[5,3],c[6,3],c[7,3],c[8,3],c[9,3],c[10,3],c[11,3],c[12,3],c[13,3])
lbls<-c("99","00","01","02","03","04","05","06","07","08","09","10")
```

Now the R script to actually produce the bar chart visualization is as follows:

```
# --- create the bar chart
barplot(bars, names.arg=lbls, col="red")
title(main = list("Smoking Patients Year to Year", font = 2))
```

The following is the generated visualization:

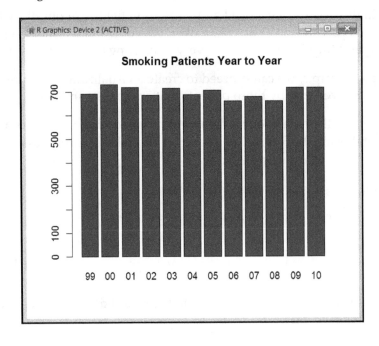

Example 2

In the preceding examples, we've presented some pretty basic and straightforward data profiling exercises. Typically, once you've become somewhat familiar with your data, having added some context (though some basic profiling), one would extend the profiling process trying to look at the data in additional ways using techniques such as the ones mentioned in the beginning of this chapter.

Defining new data points based upon the existing data, performing comparisons, looking at contrasts (between data points), identifying tendencies, and using dispersions to establish the variability of the data.

Let's now review some of these options for extended profiling using simple examples as well as the same source data that was used in the previous section examples.

Definitions and explanations

One method of extending your data profiling is to add to the existing data by creating additional definition or explanatory attributes (in other words, add new fields to the file). This means that you use existing data points found in the data to create (hopefully new and interesting) perspectives on the data.

In the data used in this chapter, a thought-provoking example might be to use the existing patient information (such as the patient's weight and height) to calculate a new point of data: **Body Mass Index (BMI)** information.

A generally accepted formula for calculating a patient's body mass index is:

BMI = (Weight (lbs.) / (Height (in))^2) x 703

Consider this example: *(165 lbs.) / (70^2) x 703 = 23.67* BMI.

Using the preceding formula, we can use the following R script (assuming we've already loaded the R object named `tmpRTable` with our file data) to generate a new file of BMI percentages and state names:

```
j=1
for(i in 2:nrow(tmpRTable))
{
  W<-as.numeric(as.character(tmpRTable[i,5]))
  H<-as.numeric(as.character(tmpRTable[i,6]))
  P<-(W/(H^2)*703)
  datas2.df[j,1]<-format(P,digits=3)
```

```
        datas2.df[j,2]<-tmpRTable[i,9]
        j=j+1
    }
    write.csv(datas2.df[1:j-1,1:2],file="C:/Big Data Visualization/Chapter
    3/BMI.txt", quote = FALSE, row.names = FALSE)
```

The following is a portion of the generated file:

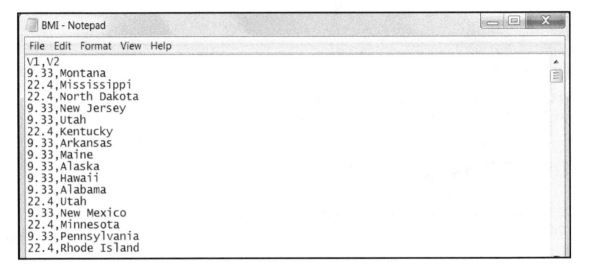

Now we have a new file of BMI percentages by state (one BMI record for each hospital visit in each state).

Earlier in this chapter, we touched on the concept of looping or reading through all of the records in a file or data source and creating counts based on various field or column values. Such logic works fine for medium or smaller files, but a much better approach (especially with big data files) would be to use the power of various R commands.

No looping

Although the R script described earlier does work, it requires looping through each record in our file, which is slow and inefficient, to say the least. So, let's consider a better approach.

Again, assuming we've already loaded the R object named tmpRTable with our data, the following R script can accomplish the same results (create the same file) in just two lines:

```
PDQ<-
paste(format((as.numeric(as.character(tmpRTable[,5]))/(as.numeric(as.charac
ter(tmpRTable[,6]))^2)*703),digits=2),',',tmpRTable[,9],sep="")
```

```
write.csv(PDQ,file="C:/Big Data Visualization/Chapter 3/BMI.txt", quote =
FALSE,row.names = FALSE)
```

We could now use this file (or a similar one) as input to additional profiling exercises or to create a visualization, but let's move on.

Comparisons

Performing comparisons during data profiling can also add new and different perspectives to the data. Beyond simple record counts (such as total smoking patients visiting a hospital versus the total non-smoking patients visiting a hospital) one might ponder to compare the total number of hospital visits for each state to the average number of hospital visits for a state. This would require calculating the total number of hospital visits by state as well as the total number of hospital visits overall (then computing the average).

The following two lines of code use the R functions table and `write.csv` to create a list (a file) of the total number of hospital visits found for each state:

```
# --- calculates the number of hospital visits for each
# --- state (state ID is in field 9 of the file
StateVisitCount<-table(datas.df[9])

# --- write out a csv file of counts by state
write.csv (StateVisitCount, file="C:/Big Data Visualization/Chapter
3/visitsByStateName.txt", quote = FALSE, row.names = FALSE)
```

The following is a portion of the file that is generated:

```
visitsByStateName - Notepad

File  Edit  Format  View  Help

ar1,Freq
,2582
 state,1
Alabama,4572
Alaska,4541
Arizona,4595
Arkansas,4624
California,4531
Colorado,4520
Connecticut,4459
Delaware,4497
Florida,4506
Georgia,2070
Hawaii,357
Idaho,1995
Illinois,2047
Indiana,2063
```

The following R command can be used to calculate the average number of hospitals by using the `nrow` function to obtain a count of records in the data source and then divide it by the number of states:

```
# --- calculate the average
averageVisits<-nrow(datas.df)/50
```

Going a bit further with this line of thinking, you might consider that the nine states the U.S. Census Bureau designates as the Northeast region are `Connecticut`, `Maine`, `Massachusetts`, `New Hampshire`, `New York`, `New Jersey`, `Pennsylvania`, `Rhode Island`, and `Vermont`. What is the total number of hospital visits recorded in our file for the northeast region?

R makes it simple with the `subset` function:

```
# --- use subset function and the "OR" operator to only have
# --- northeast region states in our list
NERVisits<-subset(tmpRTable, as.character(V9)=="Connecticut"
| as.character(V9)=="Maine"
| as.character(V9)=="Massachusetts"
| as.character(V9)=="New Hampshire"
| as.character(V9)=="New York"
| as.character(V9)=="New Jersey"
| as.character(V9)=="Pennsylvania"
| as.character(V9)=="Rhode Island"
| as.character(V9)=="Vermont")
```

Extending our scripting, we can add some additional queries to calculate the average number of hospital visits for the northeast region and the total country:

```
AvgNERVisits<-nrow(NERVisits)/9
averageVisits<-nrow(tmpRTable)/50
```

And let's add a visualization:

```
# -- the c objet is the the data for the barplot function to
# --- graph
c<-c(AvgNERVisits, averageVisits)

# --- use R barplot
barplot(c, ylim=c(0,3000),
ylab="Average Visits", border="Black",
names.arg = c("Northeast","all"))
title("Northeast Region vs Country")
```

The generated visualization is shown in the following screenshot:

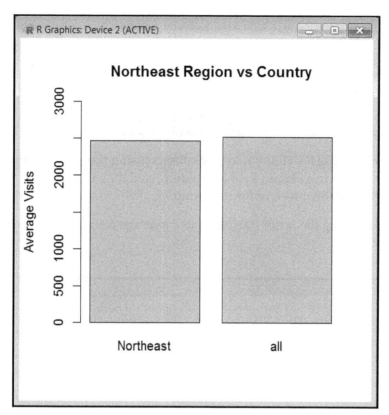

Contrasts

The examination of contrasting data is another form of extending data profiling.

For example, using this chapter's data, one could contrast the average body weight of patients that are under a doctor's care against the average body weight of patients that are not under a doctor's care (after calculating average body weights for each group).

To accomplish this, we can calculate the average weights for patients that fall into each category (those currently under a doctor's care and those not currently under a doctor's care) as well as for all patients, using the following R script:

```
# --- read in our entire file
tmpRTable<-read.table(file="C:/Big Data Visualization/Chapter
3/sampleHCSurvey02.txt",sep=",")
```

```
# --- use the subset functionto create the 2 groups we are
# --- interested in
UCare.sub<-subset(tmpRTable, V20=="Yes")
NUCare.sub<-subset(tmpRTable, V20=="No")
# --- use the mean function to get the average body weight of all pateints
in the file as well as for each of our separate groups
average_undercare<-mean(as.numeric(as.character(UCare.sub[,5])))
average_notundercare<-mean(as.numeric(as.character(NUCare.sub[,5])))
averageoverall<-
mean(as.numeric(as.character(tmpRTable[2:nrow(tmpRTable),5])))
average_undercare;average_notundercare;averageoverall
```

In short order, we can use R's ability to create subsets (using the `subset` function) of the data based upon values in a certain field (or column) and then use the `mean` function to calculate the average patient weight for the group.

The results from running the script (the calculated average weights) are shown in the following screenshot:

```
R Console
> tmpRTable<-read.table(file="C:/Big Data Visualization/Chapter 3/sampleHCSurvey02.txt",sep=",")
> UCare.sub<-subset(tmpRTable, V20=="Yes")
> NUCare.sub<-subset(tmpRTable, V20=="No")
> average_undercare<-mean(as.numeric(as.character(UCare.sub[,5])))
> average_notundercare<-mean(as.numeric(as.character(NUCare.sub[,5])))
> averageoverall<-mean(as.numeric(as.character(tmpRTable[2:nrow(tmpRTable),5])))
> average_undercare;average_notundercare;averageoverall
[1] 124.0191
[1] 117.3592
[1] 118.0215
> |
```

We can use the calculated results to create a simple visualization as follows:

```
# --- use R barplot to create the bar graph of
# --- average patient weight
barplot(c, ylim=c(0,200), ylab="Patient Weight", border="Black", names.arg
= c("under care","not under care", "all"), legend.text=
c(format(c[1],digits=5),format(c[2],digits=5),format(c[3],digits=5)))>
title("Average Patient Weight")
```

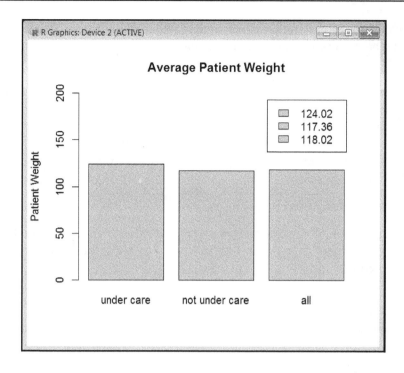

Tendencies

Identifying tendencies present within your data is also an interesting way of extending data profiling. For example, using this chapter's sample data, you might determine what the number of servings of water that was consumed per week by each patient `age` group.

Earlier in this section, we created a simple R script to count visits by age groups; it worked, but in a big data scenario, this may not work. A better approach would be to categorize the data into the age groups (age is the fourth field or column in the file) using the following script:

```
# --- build subsets of each age group
agegroup1<-subset(tmpRTable, as.numeric(V4)<22)
agegroup2<-subset(tmpRTable, as.numeric(V4)>21 & as.numeric(V4)<35)
agegroup3<-subset(tmpRTable, as.numeric(V4)>34 & as.numeric(V4)<45)
agegroup4<-subset(tmpRTable, as.numeric(V4)>44 & as.numeric(V4)<55)
agegroup5<-subset(tmpRTable, as.numeric(V4)>54 & as.numeric(V4)<66)
agegroup6<-subset(tmpRTable, as.numeric(V4)>64)
```

After we have our grouped data, we can calculate water consumption. For example, to count the total weekly servings of water (which is in field or column 96) for age group 1, we can use:

```
# --- field 96 in the file is the number of servings of water
# --- below line counts the total number of water servings for
# --- age group 1
sum(as.numeric(agegroup1[,96]))
```

Alternatively, to calculate the average number of servings of water for the same age group, we can use the following code:

```
mean(as.numeric(agegroup1[,96]))
```

 R requires the explicit conversion of the value of field 96 (even though it comes in the file as a number) to a number using the `as.numeric` R function.

Now, let's create the visualization of this perspective of our data. The following is the R script used to generate the visualization:

```
# --- group the data into age groups
agegroup1<-subset(tmpRTable, as.numeric(V4)<22)
agegroup2<-subset(tmpRTable, as.numeric(V4)>21 & as.numeric(V4)<35)
agegroup3<-subset(tmpRTable, as.numeric(V4)>34 & as.numeric(V4)<45)
agegroup4<-subset(tmpRTable, as.numeric(V4)>44 & as.numeric(V4)<55)
agegroup5<-subset(tmpRTable, as.numeric(V4)>54 & as.numeric(V4)<66)
agegroup6<-subset(tmpRTable, as.numeric(V4)>64)

# --- calculate the averages by group
g1<-mean(as.numeric(agegroup1[,96]))
g2<-mean(as.numeric(agegroup2[,96]))
g3<-mean(as.numeric(agegroup3[,96]))
g4<-mean(as.numeric(agegroup4[,96]))
g5<-mean(as.numeric(agegroup5[,96]))
g6<-mean(as.numeric(agegroup6[,96]))

# --- create the visualization
barplot(c(g1,g2,g3,g4,g5,g6),
+ axisnames=TRUE, names.arg = c("<21", "22-34", "35-44", "45-54", "55-64",
">65"))
> title("Glasses of Water by Age Group")
```

The generated visualization is shown in the following screenshot:

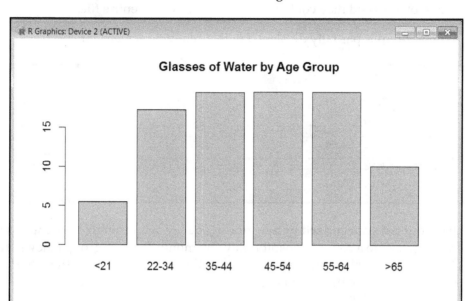

Dispersion

Finally, dispersion is still another method of extended data profiling.

Dispersion measures how various elements selected behave with regards to some sort of central tendency, usually the mean. For example, we might look at the total number of hospital visits for each age group, per calendar month in regards to the average number of hospital visits per month.

For this example, we can use the R function subset in the R scripts (to define our age groups and then group the hospital records by those age groups) like we did in our last example. The following is the script showing the calculation for each group:

```
agegroup1<-subset(tmpRTable, as.numeric(V4) <22)
agegroup2<-subset(tmpRTable, as.numeric(V4)>21 & as.numeric(V4)<35)
agegroup3<-subset(tmpRTable, as.numeric(V4)>34 & as.numeric(V4)<45)
agegroup4<-subset(tmpRTable, as.numeric(V4)>44 & as.numeric(V4)<55)
agegroup5<-subset(tmpRTable, as.numeric(V4)>54 & as.numeric(V4)<66)
agegroup6<-subset(tmpRTable, as.numeric(V4)>64)
```

Remember that the preceding scripts create subsets of the entire file (which we loaded into the `tmpRTable` object) and they contain all of the fields of the entire file.

The `agegroup1` group is partially displayed in the following screenshot:

	row.names	V1	V2	V3	V4	V5	V6	V7	V8	V9	V10
1	1	Patientid	recorddate	sex	age	weight	height	no_hospital_visits	heartrate	state	relationsh
2	14	000013	Jun/3/2009	Female	7	65	70	2	200	New Mexico	Divorced
3	15	000014	Jan/8/2013	Male	5	170	73	6	200	Minnesota	Other
4	25	000024	Nov/7/2016	Female	15	65	70	7	200	Idaho	Divorced
5	33	000032	May/7/2002	Male	14	170	73	2	200	New Jersey	5
6	43	000042	Oct/2/2008	Female	18	65	70	0	200	Arkansas	8
7	46	000045	Jan/6/2008	Female	17	65	70	9	200	Indiana	Other
8	55	000054	May/11/2009	Male	14	170	73	8	200	Indiana	Divorced
9	61	000060	Jun/2/2011	Male	15	170	73	3	200	Mississippi	Single
10	62	000061	Jul/6/2015	Male	20	170	73	3	200	South Carolina	Married

Once we have our data categorized by age group (`agegroup1` through `agegroup6`), we can then go on and calculate a count of hospital stays by month for each group (shown in the following R commands). Note that the `substr` function is used to look at the month code (the first three characters of the record date) in the file since we (for now) don't care about the year.

The `table` function can then be used to create an array of counts by month:

```
az1<-table(substr(agegroup1[,2],1,3))
az2<-table(substr(agegroup2[,2],1,3))
az3<-table(substr(agegroup3[,2],1,3))
az4<-table(substr(agegroup4[,2],1,3))
az5<-table(substr(agegroup5[,2],1,3))
az6<-table(substr(agegroup6[,2],1,3))
```

```
> az1<-table(substr(agegroup1[,2],1,3))
> az1

 re  Apr  Aug  Dec  Feb  Jan  Jul  Jun  Mar  May  Nov  Oct  Sep
  1 2139 2175 2176 2073 2074 2162 2128 2056 2123 2029 2056 2131
> |
```

Using the preceding month totals, we can then calculate an average number of hospital visits for each month using the mean R function . This will be the mean of the total for the month for ALL age groups:

```
JanAvg<-mean(az1["Jan"], az2["Jan"], az3["Jan"], az4["Jan"], az5["Jan"],
az6["Jan"])
```

 The preceding code example can be used to calculate an average for each month.

Next we can calculate the totals for each month, for each age group:

```
Janag1<-az1["Jan"];Febag1<-az1["Feb"];Marag1<-az1["Mar"];Aprag1<-
az1["Apr"];Mayag1<-az1["May"];Junag1<-az1["Jun"]
Julag1<-az1["Jul"];Augag1<-az1["Aug"];Sepag1<-az1["Sep"];Octag1<-
az1["Oct"];Novag1<-az1["Nov"];Decag1<-az1["Dec"]
```

The following code stacks the totals so we can more easily visualize it later (we would have one line for each age group (that is, Group1Visits, Group2Visits, and so on):

```
Monthly_Visits<-c(JanAvg, FebAvg, MarAvg, AprAvg, MayAvg, JunAvg, JulAvg,
AugAvg, SepAvg, OctAvg, NovAvg, DecAvg)
Group1Visits<-
c(Janag1,Febag1,Marag1,Aprag1,Mayag1,Junag1,Julag1,Augag1,Sepag1,Octag1,Nov
ag1,Decag1)
Group2Visits<-
c(Janag2,Febag2,Marag2,Aprag2,Mayag2,Junag2,Julag2,Augag2,Sepag2,Octag2,Nov
ag2,Decag2)
```

Finally, we can now create the visualization:

```
plot(Monthly_Visits, ylim=c(1000,4000))
lines(Group1Visits, type="b", col="red")
lines(Group2Visits, type="b", col="purple")
lines(Group3Visits, type="b", col="green")
lines(Group4Visits, type="b", col="yellow")
lines(Group5Visits, type="b", col="pink")
lines(Group6Visits, type="b", col="blue")
title("Hosptial Visits", sub = "Month to Month",
cex.main = 2,    font.main= 4, col.main= "blue",     cex.sub = 0.75,
font.sub = 3, col.sub = "red")
```

Now enjoy the generated output:

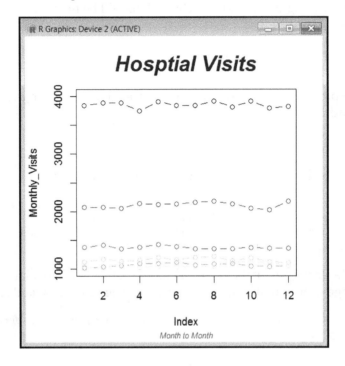

Summary

In this chapter, we went over the idea and importance of establishing context and perhaps identifying perspectives to big data, using the data profiling with R.

Additionally, we introduced and explored the R programming language as an effective means to profiling big data and used R in numerous illustrative examples.

Once again, R is an extremely flexible and powerful tool that works well for data profiling and the reader would be well served researching and experimenting with the languages and vast libraries available today, as we have only scratched the surface of the features currently available.

In the next chapter, we will dive into big data quality, using Data Manager.

4
Addressing Big Data Quality

In this chapter, we will talk about the categories of categorized data quality and the challenges big data brings to them. In addition, we will offer examples demonstrating concepts for effectively addressing these areas.

The chapter is organized into the following main sections:

- Data quality categorized
- DataManager
- DataManager and big data
- Some examples
- More examples

To make programming a bit easier, programming languages categorize data into types or a datatype. These categories of data are a defined kind or a set of possible values allowed by the type and allow progress to be made or, specifically, solutions to be crafted.

The same concept may be applied to the challenge of data quality. By understanding the categories of data quality, it makes it easier (while using an appropriate tool choice) to identify and address issues with the quality of your big data.

Data quality categorized

In early computing, the term **Garbage In Garbage Out** (**GIGO**) was popular and well known. It was meant to remind us that computers process all data without judgment. In other words, the quality of data processed by computers (or used to create data visualizations) is not guaranteed. If your data is wrong, your results will be wrong.

While what we just mentioned might be obvious, it may not be obvious that a data visualization you are reviewing was generated using data with poor quality and therefore is presenting an incorrect picture. Remember the visualization of the big dipper from Chapter 1, *Introduction to Big Data Visualization*? Imagine what it might look like when using incorrect data points:

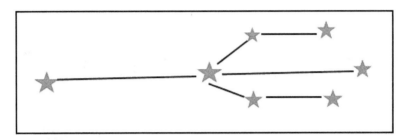

Data visualizations will only show the value if the data used to create the visualizations has had its quality assured to the appropriate level through routine and regular review and evaluation, practices that, when using large volumes of data, can become extremely demanding.

Frankly, data quality is relative as the level of accurateness or completeness is relative to or relates closely to the intended use of the data.

For example, based upon intended use, consider the following. When considering the level of data quality, one might agree that pollsters routinely determine what level of statistical confidence is required. In other words, they determine the number of people in an entire group and how accurate they want their results to be (accuracy), which then dictates the sampling technique they may use.

In Chapter 3, *Understanding Your Data Using R*, we came across a file of patient survey information, which contained over 105 fields or columns. In all of the various examples given, none required using all of these columns. When evaluating the level of data quality, keep in mind that it is not always necessary for all columns in a file to have values in them (completeness).

Time-varying datasets can be tricky. They contain information that is altered over time, due to continuously executed, time-dependent update processes or events during a time span. You might argue that you'd always want the most current data (update status), but is it as important to have up-to-the minute data when visualizing real-estate market values? How about extreme weather tracking?

And soon, hopefully, you get the picture.

From Chapter 1, *Introduction to Big Data Visualization*:

> *"The level of data quality can be affected by the way it is entered, stored, and managed and the process of addressing data quality requires a routine and regular review and evaluation of the data...".*

Being successful with addressing data quality demands an understanding of both your data (which is what we just learned from Chapter 3, *Understanding Your Data Using R*, as well as the ability to identify and resolve the issues with your data.

In Chapter 1, *Introduction to Big Data Visualization*, we recognized the most general categories of data quality; how do you address them? The first step is to have an understanding of each of them:

- **Accuracy**: There are many varieties of data inaccuracies and the most common examples include: poor math, out of range, invalid values, duplication, and more.
- **Completeness**: Data sources may be missing values from particular columns, missing entire columns, or even complete transactions.
- **Update status**: As part of your quality assurance, you need to establish the cadence of data refresh or updating as well as have the ability to determine when the data was last saved or updated. This is also referred to as latency.
- **Relevance**: This involves identification and elimination of information that you don't need or care about, given your objectives. An example would be removing sales transactions for pickles if you are intending on studying personal grooming products.
- **Consistency**: It's common to have to cross-reference or translate information across data sources. For example, recorded responses to a patient survey may require translation to a single consistent indicator to make later processing or visualizing easier.
- **Reliability**: Reliability is chiefly concerned with making sure the method of data gathering leads to consistent results. A common data assurance process involves establishing baselines and ranges and then routinely verifying that data results fall within established expectations. For example, districts that typically have a mix of both registered Democrat and Republican voters would warrant an investigation if data suddenly was 100% single partied.
- **Appropriateness**: Data is considered appropriate if it is suitable for the intended purpose; this can be subjective. For example, it's considered a fact that holiday traffic affects purchasing habits (that is, an increase in US flags in memorial day week does not indicate an average or expected weekly behavior).

- **Accessibility**: Data of interest may be watered down in a sea of data you are not interested in, thereby reducing the quality of the interesting data since it is mostly inaccessible. This is particularly common in big data projects. Additionally, security may play a role in the quality of your data. For example, particular computers might be excluded from captured logging files or certain health-related information may be hidden and not part of a shared patient data.

DataManager

There are numerous options to choose from when it comes to open source, easily obtainable and quick-start tools capable of addressing big data quality.

In this chapter, we will use DataManager. This is a program that allows you to process and manipulate data in an easy and logical manner through a flexible graphical interface.

At the time of writing, the DataManager tool used in these exercises can be obtained from `datamanager.com.au`.

DataManager reads from and writes to delimitated files (comma separated or CSV files) but also supports reading from various **Open Database Connectivity** (**ODBC**) data sources for greater flexibility.

It allows you to construct scenes of conceptual designs using simple mouse clicks. These scenes describe how your data will be processed and transformed (and all of the scenes you create can be saved and reused). As you'll see in the examples, DataManager makes use of the concept of functional nodes. With these nodes, you form a design by adding various nodes and linking them, such that the links form the flow of your data processing. All of this is done using a graphical work area (it's very much like IBM SPSS with perhaps less functionality, but it's free).

Each DataManager node performs a single function (which you can customize) on your data and once it completes that function, it passes your data to the node it is linked to (continuing until it encounters an output node).

You can use DataManager to create very straightforward designs or very complicated designs (using hundreds of nodes and multiple **Inputs** and **Output** nodes). Node functionalities available in DataManager include appending, deriving, distinction, fill, filter, merge, sample, select, and sort. Output options include distribution, histogram, **database** (**DB**), ODBC, quality, statistics, table, and XY plotting. In addition, you can execute external commands and leverage the power of **Visual Basic Script** (**VBScript**).

DataManager and big data

Although DataManager can handle very large datasets or files, it is comparable to most tools of its type, in that, when it comes to big data, it has essentially constrained your machine resources–processor speed, memory, and storage space. However, that is not to say it is not a very useable and effective tool for addressing big data quality (as well as accomplishing other objectives as well).

As with most big data scenarios, some of the big data challenges can be addressed outside of the tool but you can also be successful through leveraging features and functionalities within DataManager. In addition, using the appropriate strategies, you can overcome any limitations a machine may apply.

The examples in the upcoming sections of this chapter aim to properly illustrate some of those big data strategies as well as addressing the outlined data quality categories.

Some examples

To get started, let's assume that our data provider from Chapter 3, *Understanding Your Data Using R*, has supplied additional files to us containing patient survey information, but it has been communicated that the data quality of these files is suspect. In the following examples, we'll see what can be done to address specific concerns and improve the quality of the data.

Some reformatting

A profiling exercise from Chapter 3, *Understanding Your Data Using R*, was to time box the data to establish a time frame in which the hospital visits were recorded. Using R, we scanned the data looking at the field or column named **recorddate** and generated a list of four character years found in the file. By looking at the list we were able to establish that the data in the file ranged from 1999 through 2016.

This time, let's assume we've again scanned our data and observed that the **recorddate** field contains both four-character and two-character length years (as shown in the following screenshot):

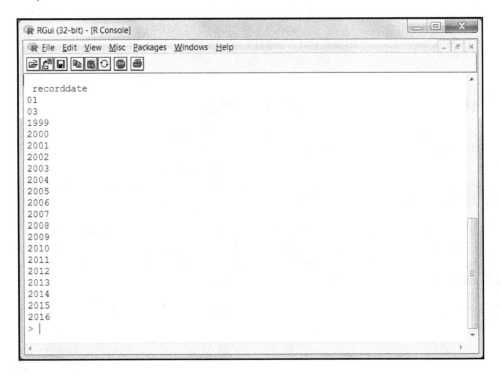

To make it a bit easier to work with the data during the process of creating data visualizations, it is always better for data to be consistent in format. Although in this example both values **01** and **2001** are valid years, to our R script, they show up as distinct values making it prone to misinterpretation. Using DataManager, we can quickly and easily reformat any two-character length record date years to the desired four-character length years (or we could convert all four-character years to two).

Let's walk-through that exercise.

A little setup

First, DataManager uses nodes to process data. There are three types of nodes defined: **Input Nodes**, **Work Nodes**, and **Output Nodes**. You define scenes connecting the nodes as logic processing streams.

Selecting nodes

Scrolling through the **Node** menu (which is always visible on the left side of DataManager), you can click on **Input Nodes** and then click on the icon named **InputFile Node**. Once you click on the node, your mouse pointer will change to the cross-hair pointer and your next mouse click (anywhere on the main work area) will drop the node you selected into the scene.

Next, repeat the same process:

1. Click on **Work Nodes** and select and add a **VBScript** node.
2. Click on **Output Nodes** and select and add a **Table** node.

Now that you have these three nodes on the main work area of DataManager, you need to connect them. The following is the screenshot of the main work area of DataManager showing a scene created with the three nodes that are selected:

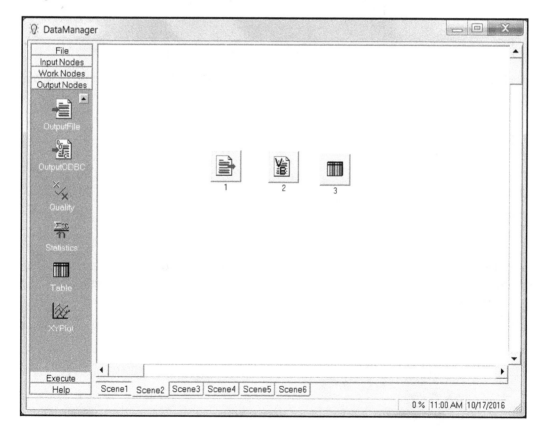

Connecting the nodes

To connect the nodes, simply right-click on the node and select **Connect Node** (shown in the following screenshot):

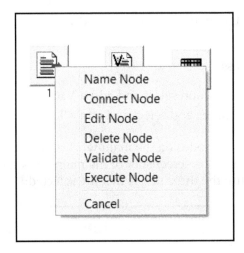

Next, click on the node you wish to connect the node to. DataManager will show the nodes connected:

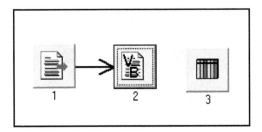

You can repeat the process to connect the **VBScript** node to the output **Table** node. Once you have all the three nodes (**Input Nodes**, **Work Nodes**, and **Output Nodes**), you can then customize the processing of the DataManager scene.

Clicking on the first node (**Input Nodes**) displays the **InputFile** dialog (shown in the following screenshot), where you can use the **Browse** button to select the file you want to process:

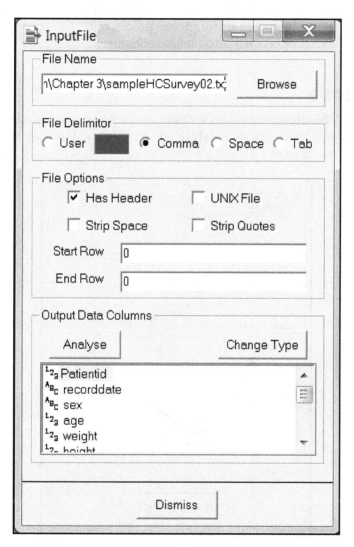

You can select **Comma** as the **File Delimitor**, and then check **Has Header** since our file includes a header row as the first record in the file. We'll explore some of the other options later in this chapter, so let's jump down and click on **Analyse**. Clicking on this button will display the fields/columns from the first record in the file. DataManager is now set up to read the entire file, record by record during scene processing. The last step in customizing these **Input Nodes** is to click on the button labeled **Dismiss**.

The work node

We've selected the **VBScript** node as our work node for this scene (shown in the following screenshot). Once again, you click on **Analyse** and the node will read in the file's header record and display the names of the fields/columns:

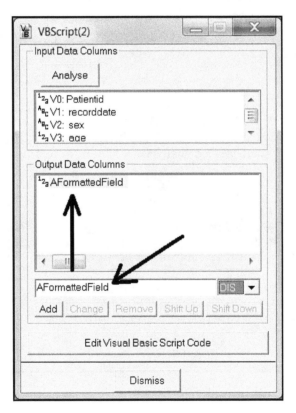

The next step in customizing the work node is to enter a name of a new field (which will hold our formatted year). Once you enter the name (I used `AFormattedField`), to the right of the new field name, you need to select the field **Type**. DataManager allows CON for continuous (numeric) and DIS for discrete (text). I selected **DIS**, since I plan to hold a four-character string value for my formatted record date year. Finally, click on the button labeled **Add** (to actually add the new field). You should now notice the new field under **Output Data Columns**.

Adding the script code

Here is the fun part, where we can do some light script programming. Click on the button labeled **Edit Visual Basic Script Code**. DataManager displays the **VBScriptCode** dialog as shown in the following screenshot:

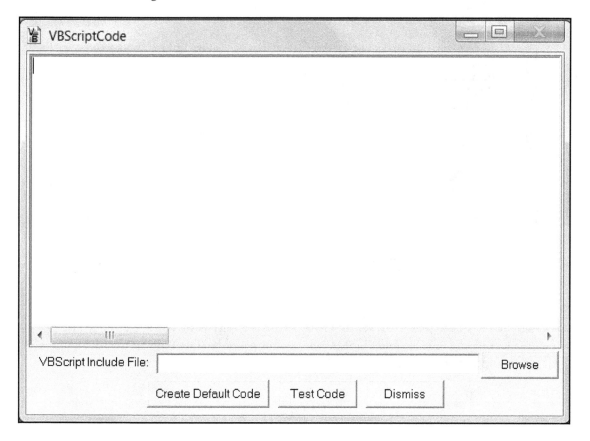

Rather than beginning to type VBScript (why waste time?), click on the button labelled **Create Default Code** and DataManager will provide a template of the script that is needed to process the data in the node (our file) to which we can add some customized logic (this is shown in the following screenshot).

The template code is explained pretty well with comments embedded in the script, so we won't go into details here, but basically the script processes our file, one record at a time. This makes it super easy for us to focus on the custom code we want and not have to recode the processing script each time we use a **VBScript** node.

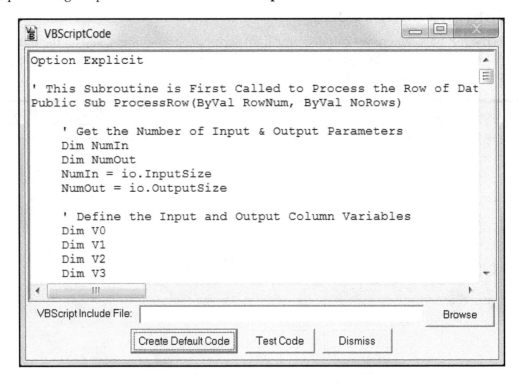

Scrolling down through the template's provided code, you will find a comment line that says `Add Your Code Here`. Under that line, I've added my code using the VBScript functions `FormatDataTime` and right to reformat the record date field into a four-character year value and then to pass back that value to the output record:

```
        ' Add Your Code Here
' --- the following code formats the record date
' --- field and then puts just the 4-character
' --- year into the new column we added

    Dim z
    z = FormatDateTime(V1,2)
    z = right(z,4)

    Out0 = z
```

A nice feature is the **Test Code** button. Click on this and DataManager will check the syntax of the **VBScriptCode** within the **VBScript** node. If it is correct, you should receive the following message:

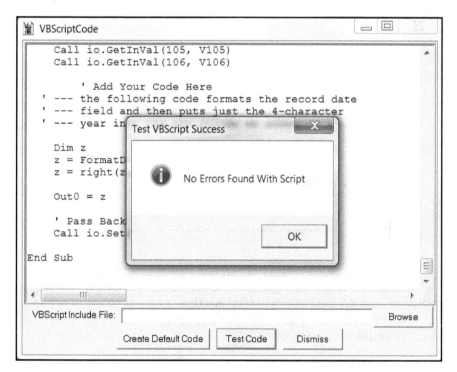

If errors exist, you'll need to correct them before proceeding. Once you receive the **No Errors** message, you can click on the button labeled **Dismiss** to dismiss and save the VBScript and then **Dismiss** (again) to close the **VBScript** node.

Lastly, we need to customize the output node. Clicking on the **Output Node**, DataManager displays the following:

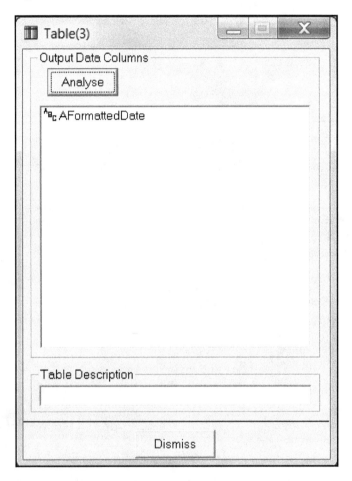

From here, you can click on the button labeled **Analyse** (similar to the previous nodes) and DataManager will list the field we added (to hold the formatted year). For this example, we can just click on **Dismiss** to close this node.

Executing the scene

Now that we have our scene (of three nodes) developed, we can execute it. To do that, we go back to the **Node** menu on the left of the DataManager workspace and click on **Execute**. This displays three icons, **Validate Run**, **Execute Run**, and **Stop** (shown in the following screenshot):

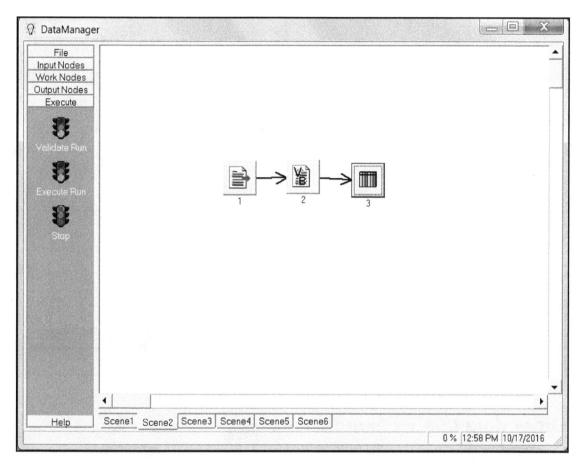

If you are unsure whether you've created the scene correctly, you can click on **Validate Run** and DataManager will validate each node and provide you with a success or failure message. Let's move on and click on **Execute Run**.

While DataManager executes your scene, you will get a visual indication of the process–the nodes will change colors as they individually execute and the DataManager status bar will display messages. Upon completion of our scene, we see the generated table of our single re-formatted field showing our years, all in YYYY format:

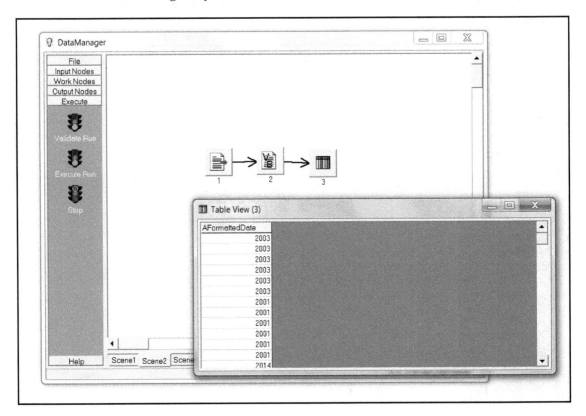

Other data quality exercises

Now that we're somewhat familiar with the basics of how DataManager works, let's look at solving some additional data quality issues.

To illustrate a few more features of DataManager, let's assume that an additional problem has been identified with our patient survey file. We have come to know that the no_hospital_visits field contains some records with no value (no response from the patient?). This is an example of when data completeness affects the quality level of the data.

It is our objective to create a data visualization showing the average number of hospital visits by a state. Using DataManager, we will use **Work Nodes** to not only identify and fill in records with missing values (for the field we are interested in) but also filter the records so that we are only working with two fields: `state` and `no_hospital_visits`.

To get started, we are assuming that we started with a new blank DataManager scene; we have added our **Input Nodes** (just like the previous example), and have customized it to read our file. In addition, rather than using the VBScript work node, we've added two new **Work Nodes** to the scene, the **Filter** node and the **Filler** node, and finally the same output mode. Again, like the previous example, we connected the nodes: **Input** | **Filter** | **Filler** | **Output**.

Now, let's look at each of the nodes' specifics. The **InputFile** dialog (shown in the following screenshot) shows that we have customized it exactly like we had in the first example:

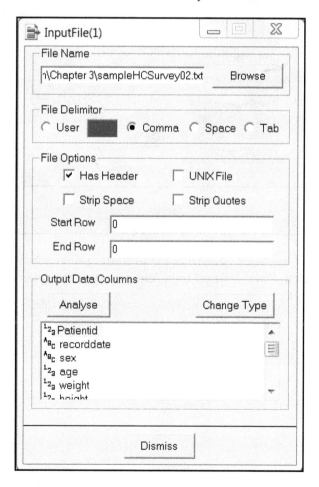

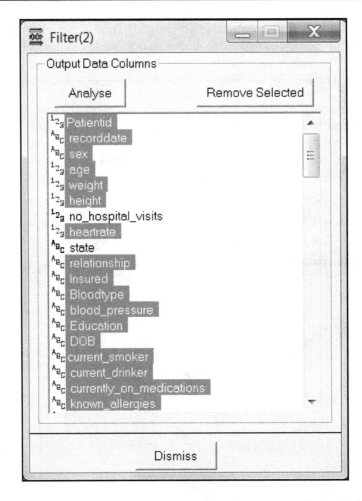

Once you have selected the fields (shown in the preceding screenshot), click on the button labeled **Remove Selected**. DataManager then removes all of the selected fields (shown in the following screenshot):

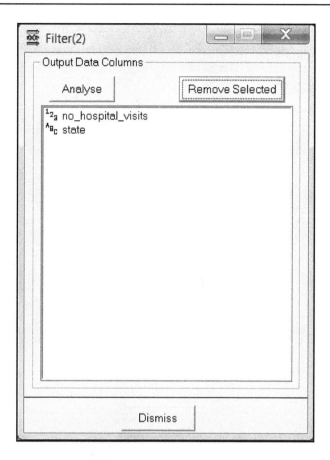

Now, click on the button labeled **Dismiss** to save our node. The **Filter** node is handy and pretty straightforward in its setup. The **Filler** node is just as handy (and easy to set up). This node allows you to fill in the missing data in all of the records in a selected column in a file. With a few clicks, you can set up the node to identify all the missing values in a column with one of the following options:

- The minimum (**Min**) value found in the column
- The maximum (**Max**) value found in the column
- The average (**Average**) value found in the column
- A user (**User**) supplied value found in the column

Click on the **Filler** node Again you can click on the button labeled **Analyse**, so DataManager lists the fields in the file that it will process with this node (in this case, the fields we set up in the previous **Filter** node: no_hospital_visits and state). This is shown in the following screenshot:

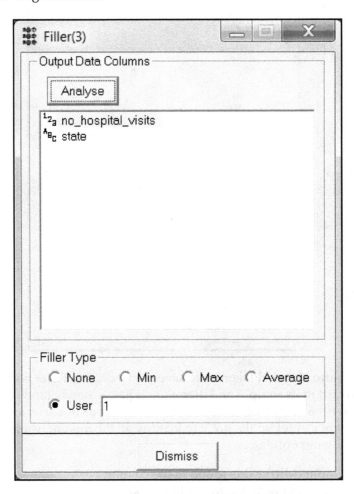

At the bottom of the **Filter** dialog, notice that I've selected **User** and then provided the value that DataManager will use to replace any missing values that are found (in the selected field).

If we execute the scene we just created, we'll end up with a list of records each containing two fields, and with the `no_hospital_visits` field fully complete (no records with missing values):

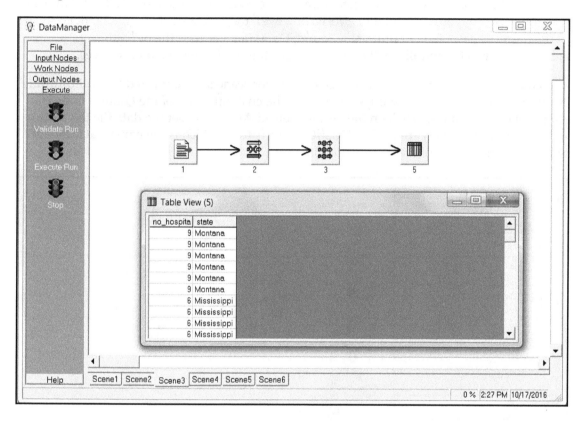

What else is missing?

On the topic of missing data, DataManager provides a **Quality** node, which displays the quality of the data based upon the data found in the columns of the data file read. This can be a time saver in your data quality efforts; however, there is one catch, missing data is NOT defined simply as a blank or null value found; DataManager uses the definition *of ? = missing data*, which, typically, is the case when dealing with most big data sources.

The **Quality** node can be added to any DataManager scene and connected to a valid **Input Nodes** (as shown in the following screenshot). The customization of the **Quality** node is simple and easy; you can click on the button labeled **Analyse** to set the data file the node will read and (optionally) provide a **Quality Description** (which is the name DataManager will give to the output of the quality node).

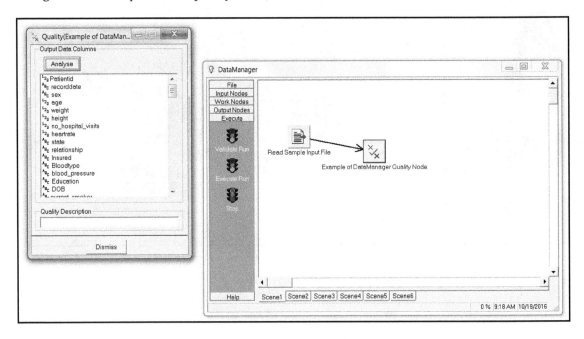

Upon executing the scene, the DataManager **Quality** node produces the following output:

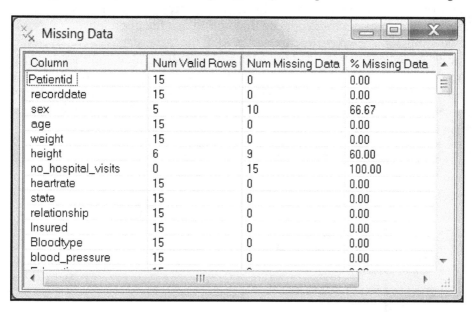

Again, to make this code work, you will need to preprocess your data, replacing various values you determine to indicate missing values (such as nulls, empty fields, and, even perhaps, zeros) with the question mark.

Status and relevance

Some simple examples of addressing the data quality topics of update status and relevance involve using the DataManager **SelectRow** and **ExecCmd** nodes.

Again, assuming a blank scene with the same **Input Nodes** (and using the same steps to connect the nodes), we can create the following processing:

Input | SelectRow | Table | OutputFile | ExecCmd

Since the **SelectRow** node is first in our scene process, let's start there. The **SelectRow** node allows you to select which rows of data you wish to process. This can address the topic or data relevance. For example, let's suppose that within our file of patient surveys we only care to review those survey records that occurred in the state of **Montana**. The **SelectRow** node makes this easy. First, we click on the select node and then the button labeled **Analyse**. As usual, DataManager lists all of the fields from the file. If we click on the field (within the fields list) named `state`, it appears at the bottom of the **SelectRow** dialog, where we can then select a logical operator (equal), type in a value to match to (`Montana`), and then an expression ender (`OUT`, which ends the expression).

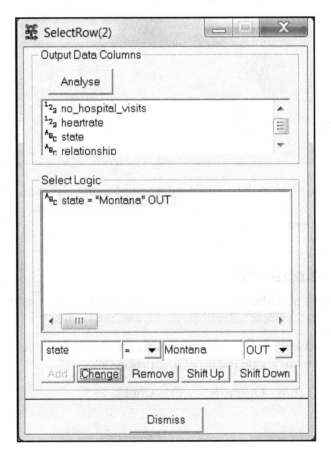

The custom logic we created here will instruct the **SelectRow** node to pass on to the next node in our scene only those records that we say are relevant–the ones where the state field value is equal to `Montana`.

In the previous examples, we used a **Table** node as our final node in the scene. This node generates a table of the records produced by your scene. In this example, we've elected to add the **OutputFile** node as the final output node. The **OutputFile** node allows you to write out a data file, based upon the parameters you set. Again, this node is pretty simple to customize, in that, you simply:

1. Provide a filename (and location) for the file you want DataManager to generate.
2. Indicate the **File Delimitor**–typically, **Comma** is selected to indicate a CSV (comma separated file).
3. Click on **Has Header** indicating that we want to include the first record as a column header file.
4. Indicate which fields will be written to our file using the (now) familiar **Analyse** button.

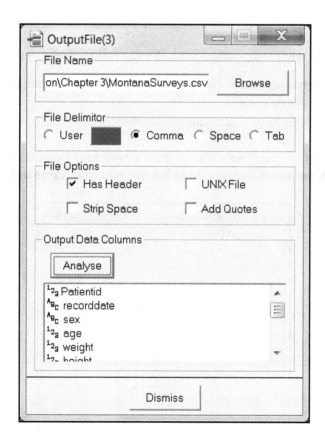

Finally, I've added the **ExecCmd** node as the final step in this scene. This node allows you to run external applications from within DataManager after an **OutputFile** node has executed to further process data or just trigger another application.

In this case, as an example, we will use this node's functionalities to execute a MS Windows script file of commands (`.cmd`) that moves our original input file to an archive location and then copies a (more recent) input file to our input location, using simple MS DOS commands such as `MOVE`:

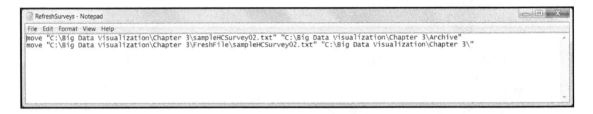

The **ExecCmd** node is also easily customized. We can follow these steps:

1. Provide the name and location of the executable file (in our example, it is `RefreshSurverys.cmd`).
2. Provide command-line run-time parameters (if any; there are none in our example).
3. Select/set any of the three options (**Run Command Executable via DOS Program**, **Wait for Command Executable to Finish**, and **Max Time to Run(Seconds)**).

- **Run Command Executable via DOS Program**: This will execute the external application in a DOS command like this:

```
command.com /c [myexternalapp.exe] [app arguments]
```

- **Wait for Command Executable to Finish**: This will instruct DataManager to wait until the external application has finished.
- **Max Time to Run (Seconds)**: This will instruct DataManager to wait for the specified time and then ask the user if they wish to terminate the external application or continue waiting for another time period. This option is only valid if the **Wait for Command Executable to Finish** is also chosen.

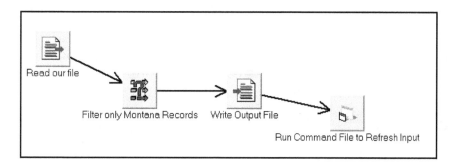

Naming your nodes

Now is a good time to mention that by right-clicking on a node you can select **Name Node** and enter a descriptive name for the node. This is highly recommended since it will be much easier to follow the processing logic of a scene when you begin working with data quality issues more complex than the simple examples given here.

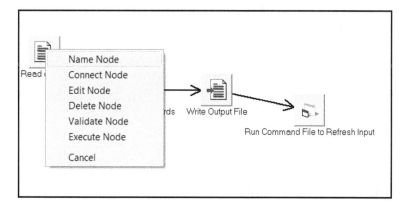

More examples

More areas where data quality may need be suspect include consistency, reliability, appropriateness, and accessibility. DataManager offers various means for addressing these as well.

Consistency

In an earlier example, we looked at the use of the DataManager **VBScript** node to reformat the record date field of our data. Another example where data may be valid yet still in constant include scenarios such as the value of the sex field.

The Male, M, Female, F, 1, or 2 values are all perhaps valid values yet these inconstant responses make visualization of data challenging. Using the **VBScript** node can easily address this example. Again, using the power and flexibility of VBScript, you might use the code shown in the following screenshot:

```
' -- code to make sex response consistent

Dim z
z = V2
IF (TRIM(z) = "M") or (TRIM(z) = "1") then
     z = "Male"
end if
IF (TRIM(z) = "F") or (TRIM(z) = "2") then
     z = "Female"
end if

Out0 = z
```

As we mentioned earlier in this chapter, it is common to have to cross-reference or translate information across data sources and the VBScript mode can be used in some cases; however, if the number of possible values are numerous (as we saw when we introduced the DataManager **Quality** node) preprocessing is most likely a better choice as there currently isn't a convenient method of testing values other than creating if logic to test each (which can easily become unsupportable).

Reliability

When it comes to reliability, one might institute a maximum (or minimum) valid value for a data point and ignore any records within a file whose value falls below or above that value.

For example, let's assume that we agree that in our patient survey data, any patient heart rate value less than the value of 27 (the lowest ever recorded, according to Guinness World Records) and higher than 299 (which would be considered pretty dangerous by most doctors) should be considered erroneous, so we want to ignore that patient survey record entirely. We could use the **VBScript** node again, but it might be easier to utilize the DataManager **SelectRow** node instead. This node allows you to set up logical expressions to determine which rows you want to pass through to the next node and which to ignore.

In the following screenshot, I've customized the **SelectRow** node with a logic statement that is based upon the `heartrate` field of our patient survey file:

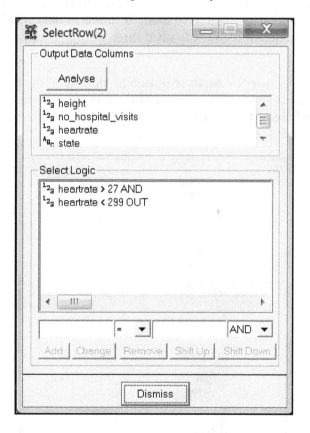

The first step was to use the button labeled **Analyse** to read in all of the fields in our file. The next step was to select (from the list of fields) heartrate, select a logical operator (< less than), provide our minimum value (27), and finally the statement continuator (AND). I repeated the process for the maximum value as **heartrate < 299 OUT** (recall that OUT terminates the logical statement).

The **SelectRow** node can then be connected to another **Work Nodes** or an **Output Nodes** to complete the intended processing.

You may see that using the **SelectRow** node is quicker than writing the actual logical statements in VBScript. Additionally, you can pretty much stack many logical statements within a single **SelectRow** node, making this node a very powerful step within the DataManager scene.

Along with this node and in support of working with big data, another node becomes quite handy, which is the **Filter** node. This node allows you to filter the input data and pass the remaining data to the output. The filtering is based on selecting which columns you wish to pass to the output. The point is if you have many columns of data within your data source, and for a particular visualization you only need three columns, why handle the unused columns?

Using the **Filter** node, you use the **Analyse** button to view all of the fields in the file and then select all of the fields you wish to remove (shown in the following screenshot). Finally, you click on **Remove Selected** and the node will be customized to only pass on (to the next node in the DataManager scene) the remaining columns.

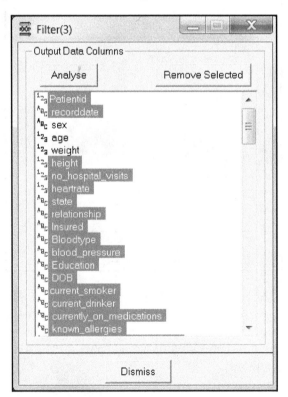

Appropriateness

Earlier in this chapter, we introduced the idea that certain data within your file may be considered inappropriate to include in a processor visualization. We have also seen how the use of the **Filter** and **SelectRow** nodes can be used to remove unwanted (inappropriate) data. Relative to the idea of selecting certain slices or subsets of your data (or of a population) aimed at a particular use is the idea of sampling your data. DataManager helps us here by providing a **Sample** node.

The DataManager **Sample** node allows you to statistically sample input rows and pass them to the next node (in the DataManager scene). The node even allows you to pass on the sampled rows as the new dataset or to remove the sampled rows and pass on the remaining as the new dataset. This node can be extremely valuable when working with big data where it may be very difficult to process all of the records provided by a data source.

To use the **Sample** node, you connect it to an **Input Nodes** and click on the button labeled **Analyse** to read into the node all of the fields within your data source, then further customize the node by:

1. Selecting a **Sample** node: **Pass on** will create a sample from your data and pass only those rows (in the sample) to the next node in the scene while **Discard** discards the sample and passes on the remaining rows (to the next node in the scene).
2. Selecting a **Style**: First we will select, at most, the number of rows given in the **Style Entry textbox**. **1 – in – N** will select only the consecutive Nth row (where **N** is the number given in the **Style Entry** textbox). Random will examine a random percentage of rows (determined by the value in the **Style Entry** textbox).

The following is an example of the customized **Sample** node:

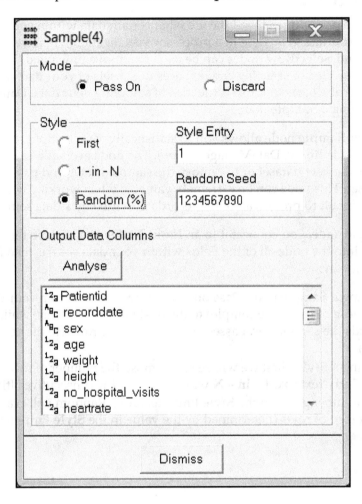

Accessibility

Finally, the quality of your data may be affected by its accessibility in whole or in part. Perhaps the specific data you need is buried within millions of rows of nonrelevant data or exists in other files that may (or may not) be formatted in the same way; in Chapter 3, *Understanding Your Data Using R*, we discussed profiling to get to know your data and put context to it. Once we have identified our data, we can use DataManager to create a high-quality file of very relevant information.

In addition to the nodes we've already reviewed in this chapter, DataManager offers the following: **Distinct**, **Append**, **Merge**, and **Sort**. These **Work Nodes** can be used to craft a single dataset that includes exactly the data you need to meet your requirements:

- The **Distinct** node: This node allows you to filter out rows that have common data values for the chosen columns. The output data from this node will contain distinct rows.
- The **Append** node: This node allows you to append two input data streams into one output data stream. The append will combine both input streams such that the **Input 1** rows will be written out followed by the **Input 2** rows, given that both input streams contain matching column types.
- The **Merge** node: This node allows you to merge two input data streams into one output data stream. The merge is performed on a row-per-row basis or by a key merge performing a left-outer-join. The method is determined on what input columns are fed into the merge node.
- The **Sort** node: This node allows you to sort the input data (row wise) based on selecting an input column. You also have a choice of sort methods.

Merging files example: Anyone who has had to merge multiple files into a single dataset will know that it is tedious work at best. With DataManager, it's a straightforward exercise.

First, you'll need an **Input** node for each of your data files set up in the same way as we did in the earlier examples in this chapter. If you have more than two files to merge, you'll need to add additional **Merge** nodes, as they are limited to merging only two files, and then merge the outputs of the first **Merge** nodes.

The **Merge** nodes are customized by simply connecting two **Input Nodes** to the **Merge** node and clicking on the button labeled **Analyse**. Optionally, you can check the **Full Left Outer Join** option on the **Output** tab of the node (shown in the following screenshot). This option allows you to specify whether the rows from **Input 1** are passed to the output when there is no match found with **Input 2** rows:

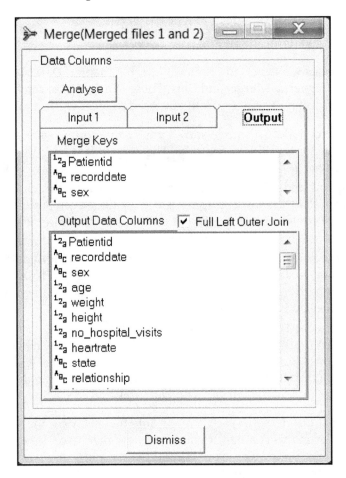

The **Input 1** tab shows what columns are fed into the **Merge** node from the first connected **Input** node and the **Input 2** tab shows what columns are fed into the **Merge** node from the second connected **Input** node. The **Output** tab shows what columns will be fed out of the node (to the next node in the DataManager scene) and also shows how the merge will be performed.

The following screenshot depicts a DataManager scene that uses the **Merge** node to merge three files into a single table:

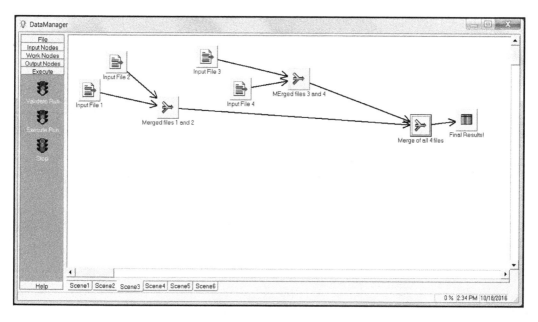

The **Merge** node can be a memory exhausting process; therefore, especially when working with big data, it is recommended that **Work Nodes** are inserted prior to merging with the objective of reducing the volume of data to be merged.

Other Output nodes

Some other interesting **Output** nodes included with DataManager include the **Distribution** node, **Histogram** node, **Statistics** node, and the **XYPlot** node. These nodes can be useful for both data profiling as well as data quality assurance.

- **Distribution** node: This node displays a distribution plot of the discrete data values contained within the chosen discrete column
- **Histogram** node: This node displays a histogram plot of the continuous data values contained within the chosen continuous column.
- **Statistics** node: This node displays statistics of the data present for the columns read by the node
- **XYPlot** node: This node displays an **XYPlot** of the chosen continuous columns

It would well be worth your time to further investigate these DataManager nodes as well as the other functionalities offered.

Summary

In this chapter, we covered some basic data quality concepts and introduced various categories for data quality. In addition, the easily obtainable and extremely useable DataManager tool was presented as a means for addressing these various data quality issues.

In the next chapter, we will get back to the business of data visualization and some of the challenges big data brings to visualization, using D3 to effectively present the results from analyses.

5
Displaying Results Using D3

Data visualization involves displaying information graphically (visually) to present a point or perspective on specific data. Beyond the simple graphs and charts in Excel, sourcing from aggregated transaction rows within a spreadsheet, today's businesses expect far more.

In this chapter, we will explore the process of visualizing data using a web browser and **Data Driven Documents (D3)** to present results from your big data analysis projects.

This chapter is organized into the following main sections:

- About D3
- D3 and big data
- Some basic examples
- More examples

About D3

D3 (or D3.js) is actually an open source JavaScript library (based upon its predecessor, the Protovis framework), designed with the intention of visualizing data using todays web standards.

D3 helps put life into your data utilizing **Scalable Vector Graphics** (**SVG**), Canvas, and standard HTML.

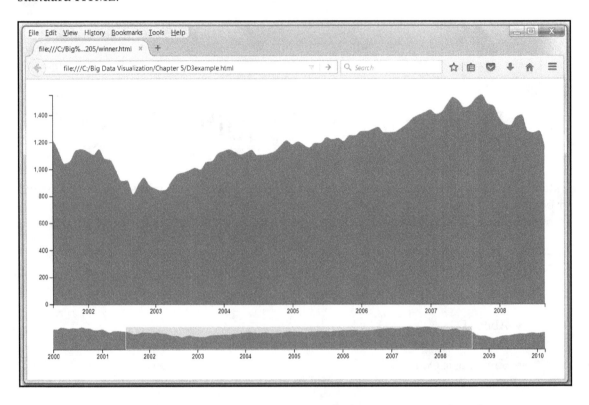

D3 combines powerful visualization and interaction techniques with a data-driven approach to DOM manipulation, giving you the full capabilities of modern browsers and the freedom to design the right visual interface for your data.

In contrast to many other libraries, D3.js allows inordinate control over the visualization of your data. Its development was noted in 2011, as version 2.0.0 was released in August 2011.

D3 is embedded within an HTML webpage, and uses prebuilt JavaScript functions to select elements, create SVG objects, style them, or add transitions, dynamic effects, and so on.

Detailed information, including the D3.js libraries can be accessed at https://D3js.org.

D3 and big data

First, let me say that you can easily bind or use your large datasets to common SVG objects using the functions available in the D3.js libraries.

The data can even be in a variety of formats, most commonly JSON, **comma-separated values (CSV)**, or **geoJSON**, but, if required, JavaScript functions can be written to read other data format.

However, large isn't big in the sense of big data. Realistically, binding a CSV file of 500 records cannot be likened to binding it to a file of 500,000 records.

So, can D3 really help in the context of big data?

Since it is low-level, D3 may seem like a bad fit for big data visualization projects. The D3.js libraries just won't work with gigabytes of data, but once you perform some preprocessing on the data, D3 can help make sense of the results.

In fact, in each of the previous chapters of this book, Chapter 2, *Access, Speed, and Storage with Hadoop*, (where we loaded data into a Hadoop environment and then used Hive to manipulate that data into workable summaries), Chapter 3, *Understanding Your Data Using R*, (where we used the power of R scripting to profile the data into meaningful summaries for visualizations), and, Chapter 4, *Addressing Big Data Quality* (where we utilized DataManager to address the quality of the data so it could be visualized) we used the following strategy:

- Assembling the data
- Profiling the data
- Addressing quality concerns
- Processing for visualization, that is, summarize or aggregate, and so on
- Visualizing!

So, let us now move on–and look at some pretty interesting examples of visualizing big data using the power offered by opened sourced, D3.

Some basic examples

Just to get us underway, let's take another look at an example we used in this book's
Chapter 3, *Context – Understanding Your Data Using R*.

In that scenario, we had used some simple R scripting to summarize patient survey
information into a result or summarized a file showing a total for the number of visits for
each state in the United States. Now, using that same data file, perhaps we can get a general
idea of what D3 may be able to do for us in the form of valuable data visualization.

We'll get into the details in the next section, but for now, all we need to do to get started is
to create an HTML page based upon a bubble chart template downloaded from the D3
website (this particular template utilizes the D3 flare class libraries to create a bubble chart
from our data file).

A **bubble chart** is an interesting way to display data in an efficient, reasonable way since, in
this example, we want to show all 50 states from our data, it can be represented in a clear
fashion.

The following figure shows the resulting bubble visualization generated by the D3 library
and bubble template (viewed with a web browser):

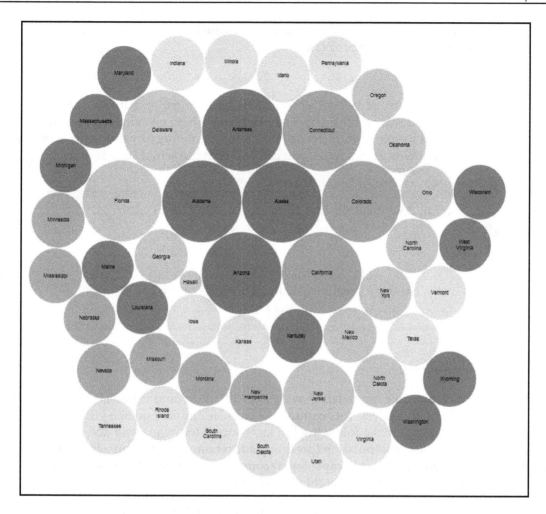

Getting started with D3

As this book does not intend to be a lecture on the interworking's of D3 (rather focusing on the use of D3 as an option to visualize big data), we will simply point out here a bit of basic information around the reader's efforts into getting started with using D3:

- The website may be found at `https://D3js.org`
- The latest version (at the time of writing) is V4.2.8, and that version can be downloaded from the following link:

  `https://github.com/D3/D3/releases/download/v4.2.8/D3.zip`

- You can simply link directly to the latest release libraries by inserting the following line in your projects:

```
<script src="https://D3js.org/D3.v4.min.js"></script>
```

Based on your environment, or at least while you are experimenting with the D3 examples, I recommend that you download the actual source files so that you can use a local reference (shown as follows), as it eliminates the possibility of encountering any problems accessing the D3 libraries (and, if you are inclined, you can see what the actual code is doing):

```
<script src="D3.v4.min.js"></script>
```

You can download the files from: `https://github.com/D3/D3`.

Finally, there are great instructional tutorials offered at: `https://github.com/D3/D3/wiki/Tutorials`.

Now, on to the examples!

When we talk of visualizing big data, what we actually mean (and expect) is visualizing the aggregated results of an analysis (no, contrary to popular opinion, no one visualizes raw big data directly). To this point, the following is a key concept to understand and embrace that the capture and storing, manipulation (profiling, addressing quality, and aggregating), and visualizing are all separate (and encapsulated) components and can (and most likely should) each be addressed with different tools or technologies.

This way, each component leverages the tool that is just right for the particular purpose.

In the following example, we are dealing with manufacturing data. Specifically, we have data captured from a number of machines at a particular plant utilizing a data logging system. The **data logger** is a program that gathers production-line data and writes it to a log file. In this scenario, the data logger is installed on each manufacturing machine. The data logger collects production data directly from the machine, stores it in memory, and periodically sends it off to the data repository (a log file). In the event of a network outage, the onboard data logger can continue to collect production information from the machine while the network is down and then back-fill the data to the log file when the network comes back up. This results in millions of machine transaction status records accumulating daily, a big data scenario for sure.

The transaction records contain the following information:

Date/Time	**This is the exact date and time of day that the transaction log record was captured.**
Shift ID	The plant runs three shifts, so this would be 1, 2, or 3.
Machine ID	The plant has five machines in operation; 001, 002, 003, 004, and 005.
Part count	Numeric total of products produced by the machine since the previous polling cycle.
Machine state	The machine state is the current condition of the machine. Typical states are running, idle, unplanned down, and planned down, changeover/setup, and offline.
Error code	These error codes can be automatically generated by the controller on the machine or can correspond to a list of downtime reasons that are manually selected by the machine operator.

The following screenshot shows a sample of the raw data records:

```
samplePlanData - Notepad
File  Edit  Format  View  Help
Date_Time,Shift,Machine_ID,Part_Count,Machine_State,Error_Code
1/14/2012 7:43:30 AM,First,0003,2363,Running,0
1/1/2012 7:27:25 AM,Third,0005,7692,Running,0
1/17/2012 7:27:11 AM,First,0004,7455,Running,0
1/16/2012 8:01:32 AM,Third,0002,7170,Running,0
1/4/2012 8:30:59 AM,First,0005,2062,Running,0
1/2/2012 7:24:19 AM,First,0002,3780,Running,0
1/5/2012 7:57:33 AM,Second,0002,6218,Running,0
1/3/2012 7:01:49 AM,Third,0004,2377,Running,0
1/8/2012 8:14:26 AM,Third,0004,136,Running,0
1/21/2012 8:16:01 AM,Second,0001,7561,Running,0
1/18/2012 7:23:49 AM,Third,0002,2605,Running,0
1/12/2012 7:29:11 AM,Third,0005,1804,Running,0
1/20/2012 8:30:53 AM,First,0003,5410,Running,0
1/4/2012 8:09:46 AM,Third,0002,1473,Running,0
1/13/2012 7:31:26 AM,First,0001,663,Running,0
```

In this example, we'll skip over the process of manipulating the raw data, assuming we have performed some profiling of the data, addressed any quality issues, and formed an aggregation of the data that we wish to base our visualization upon (or drive the data from).

What we've come up with is a simple comma-delimited text file (we named it `data.csv`) with the total number of products produced for each machine ID, broken out by shift:

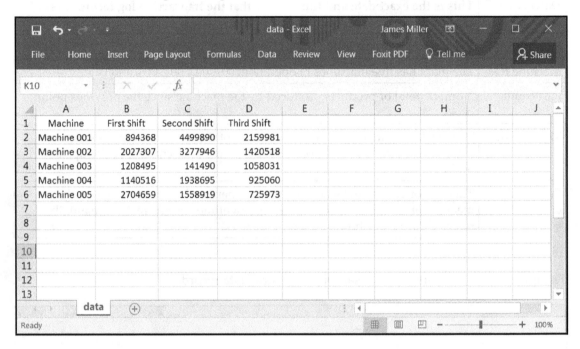

Again, one of the already available D3 visualization sample templates can be used to create a grouped bar chart. Assuming you have already downloaded the D3 libraries, the steps to adopt the template and create our visualization are as follows:

1. Download the grouped bar HTML template document.
2. Open the document in any HTML editor (or any programmer's editor).
3. Under the document's `<body>` tag, enter or modify the following code:

```
<body>
<! --- added a simple heading -->
<h1><center>Total Parts by Shift</cellspacing></h>
<! --- local include for D3 libraries -->
<script src="D3.v3.min.js"></script>
```

4. What this modification does is to add text (`Total Parts by Shift`) to be used as our visualization's heading and changes the reference to the D3 libraries (the `src= D3.v3.min.js`) to be a local reference.

5. Next, again assuming our data file is in the same local location as our HTML file, we can find the document's file reference (D3.csv) and verify the filename:

```
<!--- here is the data -->
D3.csv("data.csv", function(error, data) {
```

Once we've saved the updated HTML document, we can view it using any web browser.

Voila! We've created our first big data visualization using D3:

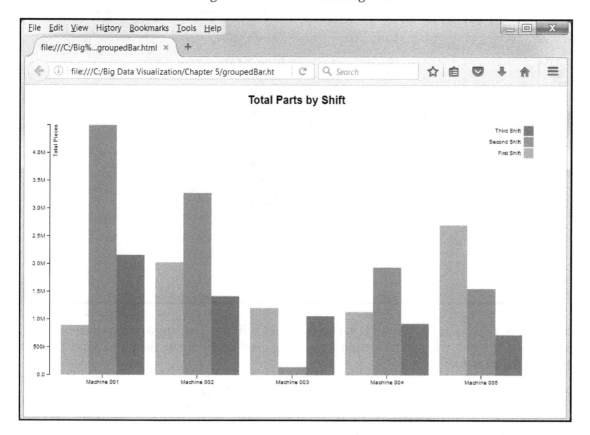

If you take a few minutes and review the extensive visual gallery available (at least at the time of writing) at https://github.com/D3/D3/wiki/Gallery, you will be able to see literally hundreds of D3 template samples showing virtually any kind of visualization you may want, all available to adopt (download, modify, and use).

Let's look at some more examples, digging deeper into the specifics of D3 use.

Another area of interest at our manufacturing plant is shift performance. Management wants to determine how the different shifts contribute to overall profitability or perhaps how each individual shift compares to the others. To do this, there are several **key performance indicators** (**KPIs**) to be scrutinized. One such indicator is total parts delivered by shift. Again, the process will be to take our big data source of raw plan records and aggregate them into a usable form.

The following screenshot shows a portion of our raw data:

```
samplePlanData - Notepad                                    _  □  X

File  Edit  Format  View  Help
Date_Time,Shift,Machine_ID,Part_Count,Machine_State,Error_Code
1/14/2012 7:43:30 AM,First,0003,2363,Running,0
1/1/2012 7:27:25 AM,Third,0005,7692,Running,0
1/17/2012 7:27:11 AM,First,0004,7455,Running,0
1/16/2012 8:01:32 AM,Third,0002,7170,Running,0
1/4/2012 8:30:59 AM,First,0005,2062,Running,0
1/2/2012 7:24:19 AM,First,0002,3780,Running,0
1/5/2012 7:57:33 AM,Second,0002,6218,Running,0
1/3/2012 7:01:49 AM,Third,0004,2377,Running,0
1/8/2012 8:14:26 AM,Third,0004,136,Running,0
1/21/2012 8:16:01 AM,Second,0001,7561,Running,0
1/18/2012 7:23:49 AM,Third,0002,2605,Running,0
1/12/2012 7:29:11 AM,Third,0005,1804,Running,0
1/20/2012 8:30:53 AM,First,0003,5410,Running,0
1/4/2012 8:09:46 AM,Third,0002,1473,Running,0
1/13/2012 7:31:26 AM,First,0001,663,Running,0
1/29/2012 8:05:51 AM,Second,0004,8990,Running,0
1/4/2012 7:24:56 AM,First,0005,907,Down,3
```

Since we've already worked with R in this book, we will use it again to manipulate our raw plant data. The following is the simple R scripting used to aggregate the part counts by shift ID to a summary file:

```
# --- reads the raw file into a R table named "parts"
parts<-read.table(file="C:/Big Data Visualization/Chapter
5/samplePlanData.txt",sep=",")
data.df <- data.frame(parts)

# --- create a subset of the raw data for each shift id
FirstShift<-subset(data.df,data.df[,2]=="First")
SecondShift<-subset(data.df,data.df[,2]=="Second")
ThirdShift<-subset(data.df,data.df[,2]=="Third")

# --- aggregate part totals by shift ID
sum(as.numeric(FirstShift[,4]))
```

```
sum(as.numeric(SecondShift[,4]))
sum(as.numeric(ThirdShift[,4]))

# --- create a summary file for visualization
sink("C:/Big Data Visualization/Chapter 5/data.tsv")
cat("shiftid")
cat("\t")
cat("partcount")
cat("\n")
cat(paste("First Shift", "\t", sum(as.numeric(FirstShift[,4]))),sep = "\t",
collapse = NULL)
cat("\n")
cat(paste("Second Shift", "\t", sum(as.numeric(SecondShift[,4]))),sep =
"\t", collapse = NULL)
cat("\n")
cat(paste("Third Shift", "\t", sum(as.numeric(ThirdShift[,4]))),sep = "\t",
collapse = NULL)
cat("\n")
sink()
```

Reminder: as we mentioned in `Chapter 3`, *Understanding Your Data Using R*, there are many approaches to using R and the previous script is just one approach. The reader is invited to use it or improve it.

The following screenshot shows the aggregated or summary file (named `data.tsv`) that the R script generates:

This summary file is then the source of our D3 data visualization (shown in the following figure):

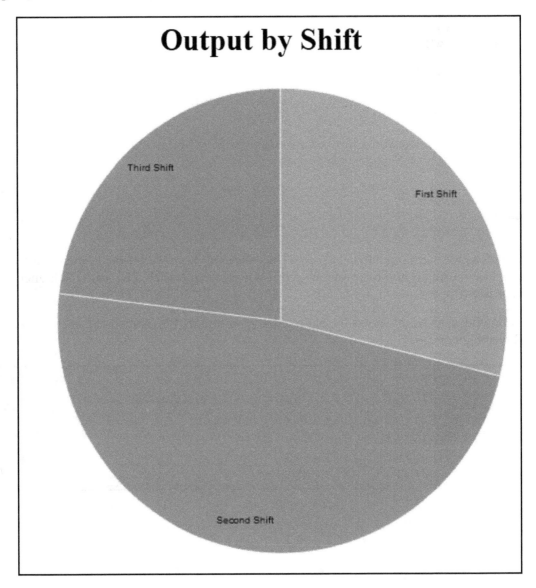

This visualization is generated using the minimalist pie chart D3-shape sample template.

To display the (preceding) visualization, the following HTML document was used (our changes are highlighted):

```
<!DOCTYPE html>
<meta charset="utf-8">
<!-add the heading -->
<h1><center>Output by Shift</center></h1>
<canvas width="960" height="500"></canvas>
<!-local reference to D3 libraries --->
<script src="D3.v4.0.0-alpha.4.min.js"></script>
<script>
var canvas = document.querySelector("canvas"),
    context = canvas.getContext("2d");

var width = canvas.width,
    height = canvas.height,
    radius = Math.min(width, height) / 2;

var colors = ["#ff8c00", "#8a89a6", "#d0743c", "#6b486b", "#a05d56",
"#d0743c", "#ff8c00"];

var arc = D3.arc()
    .outerRadius(radius - 10)
    .innerRadius(0)
    .context(context);

var labelArc = D3.arc()
    .outerRadius(radius - 40)
    .innerRadius(radius - 40)
    .context(context);

var pie = D3.pie()
    .sort(null)
    .value(function(d) { return d.partcount; });

context.translate(width / 2, height / 2);

<-- read our summary file-->
D3.requestTsv("data.tsv", function(d)
{
  d.partcount = +d.partcount;
  return d;
}, function(error, data)
{
  if (error) throw error;
  var arcs = pie(data);
  arcs.forEach(function(d, i)
  {
```

```
    context.beginPath();
    arc(d);
    context.fillStyle = colors[i];
    context.fill();
});
context.beginPath();
arcs.forEach(arc);
context.strokeStyle = "#fff";
context.stroke();
context.textAlign = "center";
context.textBaseline = "middle";
context.fillStyle = "#000";
arcs.forEach(function(d)
{
var c = labelArc.centroid(d);
context.fillText(d.data.shiftid, c[0], c[1]);
});
});
</script>
```

A little down time

Another prospective opportunity for visualization of our raw plant data is around down time. In our raw data file, there is a field named `Machine_State`. The machine state is the current condition of the machine, typically running, idle, unplanned down, planned down, changeover/setup, and offline.

In this scenario, we want to have a total count of the number of times each machine (001 through 005) recorded or wrote a transaction record where the machine was not in a running state and we'd like to see these numbers broken down by a quarter.

Searching the D3 site, we find that there is a fine stacked bar sample template that lends itself nicely to our requirements. This visual also demonstrates the use of runtime reconfiguration in that it uses a standard HTML radio button that the user can use to switch or transition the visualization view from a stacked bar to a multiples bar display format.

The template is named **Stacked-to-Multiples** and it can be found at `http://blocks.org/mb ostock/4679202` (the following figure points out the HTML radio buttons in the upper right):

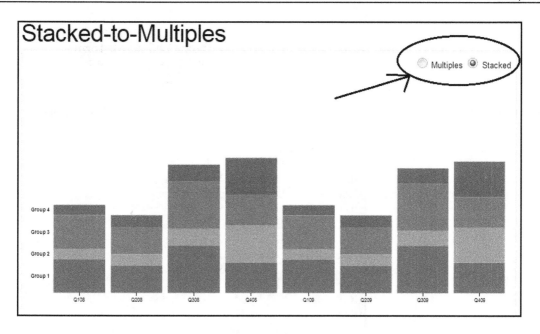

Once again, this D3 sample template uses a summarized data file to drive the visualization. The data file (named `data.tsv`) contains records with three fields: **group**, **date**, and **value**, and it is (partially) shown in the following screenshot:

group	date	value
1	2008-01	10
1	2008-04	8
1	2008-07	14
1	2008-10	9
1	2009-01	10
1	2009-04	8
1	2009-07	14
1	2009-10	9
2	2008-01	3
2	2008-04	3.5
2	2008-07	5
2	2008-10	11
2	2009-01	3
2	2009-04	3.5
2	2009-07	4.5

data.tsv

This is a pretty straightforward example that we can adapt for our purposes without much effort. First, we can pre-process our raw plant data into the preceding file format–but with one slight difference: rather than using a group field, we'll use that first field (or column) of data as our machine ID (the other two fields can remain the same).

I have also named our data file as `datastacked.tsv`, and it is partially shown here:

```
machine  date      value
001      2008-01   10
001      2008-04   8
001      2008-07   14
001      2008-10   9
001      2009-01   10
001      2009-04   8
001      2009-07   14
001      2009-10   9
002      2008-01   3
002      2008-04   5|
002      2008-07   5
002      2008-10   11
002      2009-01   3
002      2009-04   2
002      2009-07   4
```

Once again, the pre-processing of the raw plant data could be accomplished using *R* scripts or other tools. Big data sources would typically be (perhaps) chunked or processed in segments to effectively arrive at the desired aggregated or summarized file, ready for visualization. As we saw in `Chapter 3`, *Understanding Your Data Using R*, offers the ability to easily aggregate data and then merge the multiple aggregated files into a single file for visualization.

The next step (in adopting this D3 sample template) is to download the sample template and save it as an HTML document. From there, we can make a few minor modifications:

1. As mentioned earlier in this chapter, I have downloaded and saved the D3 library files, so I need to change the `src=` reference within the HTML document (to make it a local reference). It should look as follows:

```
<script src="D3.v3.min.js"></script>
```

2. Since I renamed the data file, locate the line in the HTML document referencing the file name and change it to reflect our data file name:

```
D3.tsv("datastacked.tsv", function(error, data) {
```

3. Finally, since we've changed the first field name in our data file (from group to machine), we need to change all references to that field within the HTML document. Hint: a simple global find and replace in a text editor does the trick!

4. Save the updated HTML file and view it in your web browser!

The following figure shows our data visualization showing the stacked view:

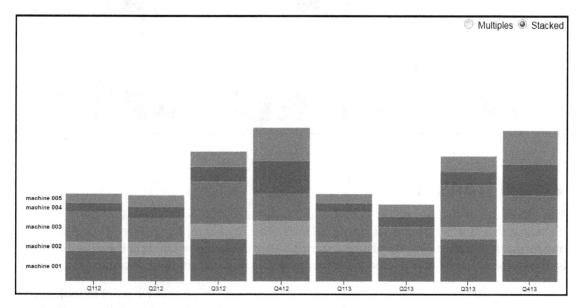

If you click on the radio button labeled **Multiples**, the visualization changes format:

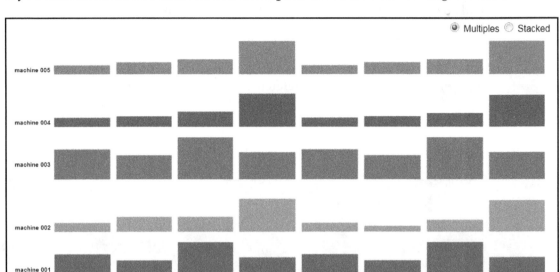

Visual transitions

The procedure of clicking on the HTML radio buttons to change the format of the visualization is known as **transitioning**. In the preceding example, we transitioned from one format to another. We can also use transitioning to change what data the visualization is driven from. Let us take a look at another example to illustrate this concept.

Going back to our manufacturing plant's raw data, let's suppose that we want to look at the output (total part count) by machine ID and by shift. We'd like to build a data visualization that displays each machines part count (its output) broken out by shift. We also want the ability to change the shift and see the visualization update (transition) appropriately.

For this example, I elected to use a D3 sample template that builds a donut pie chart (which you can find at `http://blocks.org/mbostock/5681842`). This template transitions the visualization between **Apples** data and **Oranges** data:

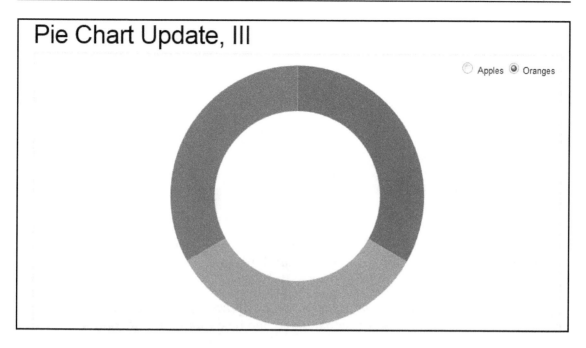

Another thought-provoking feature of this template is that it handles missing data by filling in the null or missing values with zeros (you could use any default value instead of zeros). We will examine this feature shortly.

To adopt this sample template for our purposes, we will go about following the usual steps: download the HTML template, locate and change the D3 library reference, and update the data.

Let's look at the three specific customizations:

1. I added a simple heading:

```
<center><H1>Parts by Shift</H1></center>
```

2. I modified the HTML form, changing it from apples and oranges to indicate our three plant shifts. Note that I had to add a third HTML radio button:

```
<form>
  <label><input type="radio" name="dataset" value="first"
    checked>First Shift
  </label>
  <label><input type="radio" name="dataset" value="second">Second
    Shift
  </label>
```

```
<label><input type="radio" name="dataset" value="third">Third
    Shift
</label>
</form>
```

3. I modified the function that handles missing data to validate all three shifts:

```
function type(d)
{
    d.first = +d.first || 0;
    d.second = +d.second || 0;
    d.third = +d.third || 0;
    return d;
}
```

Again, notice that I simply changed the references from `apples` and `oranges` to first and second, and then added a third reference, for our third shift.

The last step is to pre-process our raw plant data into a summary file that this D3 template can use. It is a pretty simple file, with just two fields, **apples** and **oranges** (shown in the following screenshot). You will notice that the second field (**oranges**) is missing values:

data.tsv

apples	oranges
53245	200
28479	
19697	200
24037	
40245	200

For our data, we will have three fields (one for each shift): **first**, **second**, and **third**. After having summarized our data, we see the following:

first	second	third
53245	53245	53245
28479	8479	38400
19697	28479	200
24037	1920	
40245	90000	1200

Each record in our summary file indicates a summary record for a particular machine ID with a part count for each of the three shifts. Notice that within our data, machine 004 was offline or down during the third shift so we are missing a value for that time. This will prove to be a good test for the function we modified (to handle missing values).

Once we update our HTML document one last time to reflect our summarized file name, we can open it in our web browser.

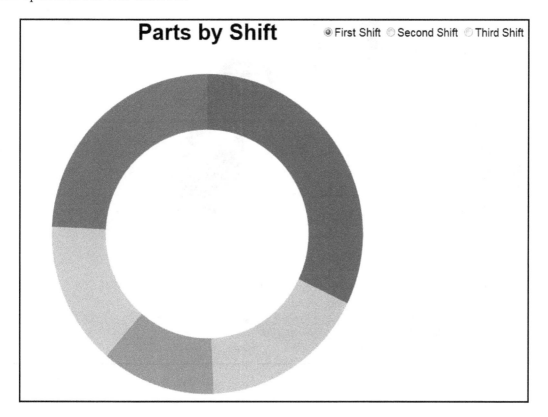

Now we see a donut pie split by machines for the first shift, but if we click on the radio button to **Change the shift** to **Second Shift**, we see the following:

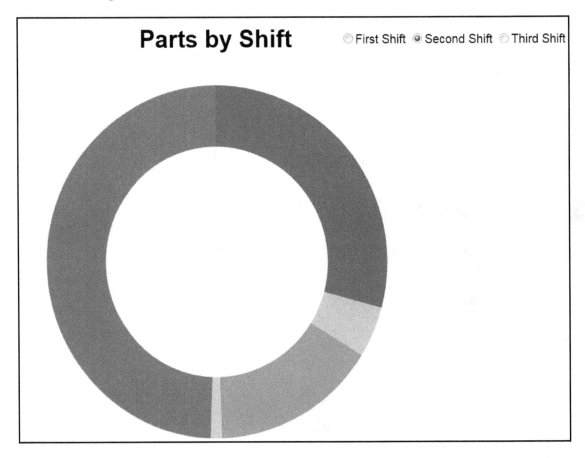

The third shift looks as follows:

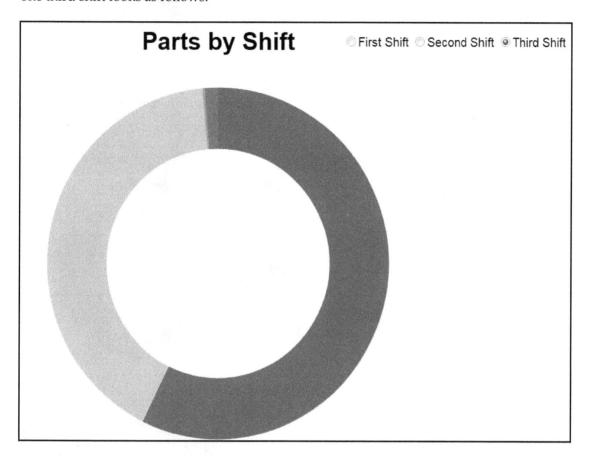

You will notice that for the third shift, machine 004 is not represented (there are only four colors shown in the chart), since it was offline and had no part count in the file.

Multiple donuts

Another interesting and perhaps useful available D3 visualization sample template is the **Sized Donut Multiples** template. This template can be viewed and downloaded from: `http://blocks.org/mbostock/4c5fad723c87d2fd8273` and it shows multiple donuts that are sized so that the area of each donut is proportionate to a total number such that the area of the donut arcs is comparable across all donuts.

In the template, the example uses a summarized data file of state populations, broken out by age group. The file is a comma-delimited file. The example uses the first field (state) as the key to determine the number of donuts to show and the total for each key indicates the size of the donut.

The example D3 visualization is shown in the following figure:

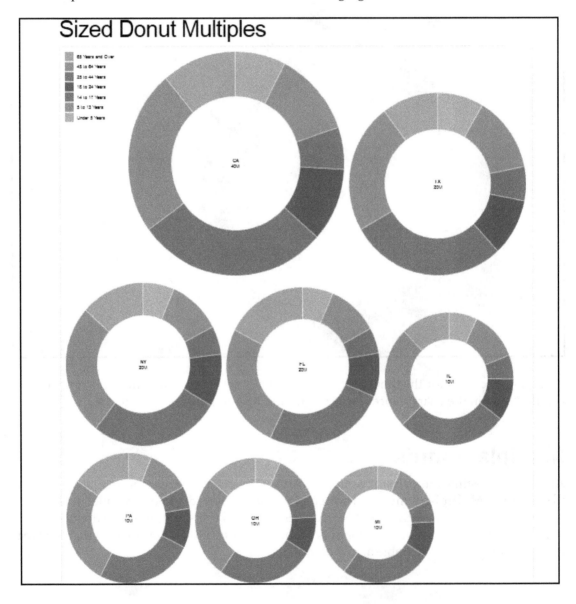

We can easily modify this template to work for us. Instead of states and population totals by age group, we will visualize machines and total parts by shift.

I've pre-processed our raw plant data again, this time creating a summary file of four columns:

- Machine
- First shift
- Second shift
- Third shift

The file has five rows of data, one for each machine. Our summary file looks as follows:

```
machine,first shift,second shift, third shift
0001,310504,552339,259034,450818,1231572
0002,52083,85640,42153,74257,198724
0003,515910,828669,362642,601943,1804762
0004,202070,343207,157204,264160,754420
0005,2704659,4499890,2159981,3853788,10604510
```

Using the same process to adopt the sample template that we have used for all of the examples throughout this chapter, we:

1. Download the sample template and save it as an HTML document.
2. Change the `src=` reference (to a local reference for the D3 libraries).
3. Change the name of the data file.
4. Add a heading.

In this example, since the D3 sample template uses the first field in the file by name (and that name is used as the visualization key), we need to again make a global change of all references to the word state to the machine.

Once you have completed the preceding changes, we can view our visualization (in a web browser):

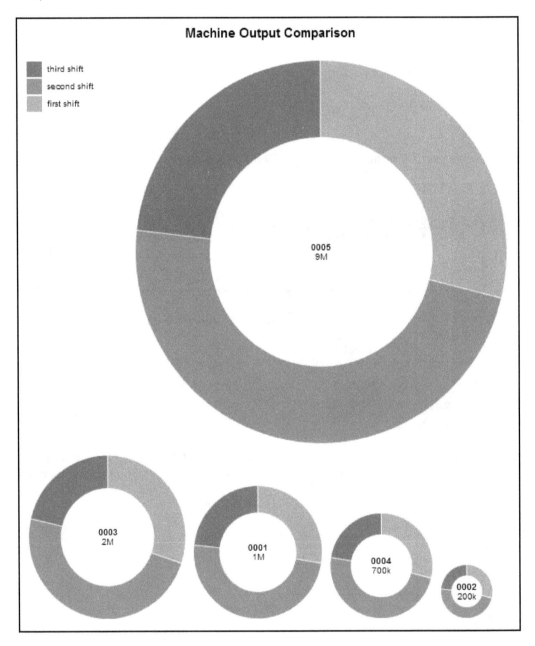

You should notice that this visualization adds a legend to each donut, which shows the machine ID or name (for example, **0005**) and the rounded total number of parts with a suffix of M for millions or K for thousands). There is also a specific donut for each machine ID and from the visualization shown, we can see that machine **0005** is the largest contributor of total parts overall (followed by machines **0003**, **0001**, **0004**, and then **0002**).

More examples

Let us now go a bit further into D3 by looking at some additional examples.

Another twist on bar chart visualizations

A bar chart is a pretty common type of data visualization and we've already seen some examples using the D3 libraries. One more bar-chart D3 template is worth a quick look. This one is able to handle negative values. Think about it–most bar charts show positive values so flipping the tic of an axis (as its referred to) requires some special logic.

The D3 example named *Bar Chart with Negative Values II* handles this kind of scenario nicely and it can be viewed and downloaded from the following location:
`http://blocks.org/mbostock/79a82f4b9bffb69d89ae`.

This sample template shows both negative and positive values for the letters **A** through **H**, and it is shown in the following figure:

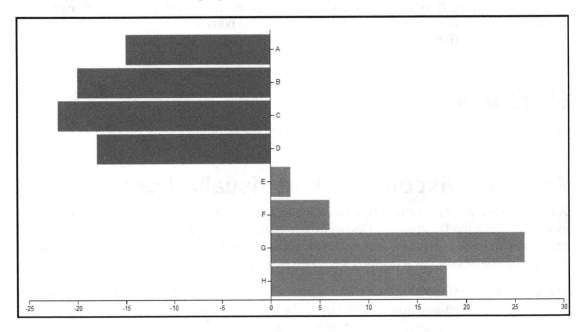

Getting back to our manufacturing plant, a new challenge has been implemented by management. That is a product output target has been set for each of the plant's machines. Management wants to monitor each machines ability to hit the target and see any deltas to the target. In other words, at any given time how does the machines part count compare to the target number?

Instead of the eight letters, we want to display our five machines and a horizontal bar showing each machines output compared to the target. So, if we use the previous visualization, machines may have a value of zero, indicating that the machine has hit the target (and there is no delta or difference between the machines part count and the target number), a positive value if that machine has surpassed the targeted total, or even a negative value if the output is less than the targeted value. Since the initial targeted value was set low, management is hoping to see all positive values, of course.

Again, adopting the sample D3 template is an easy process. Really, the key to leveraging the sample D3 templates is to first understand the format of the data that is driving the particular visualization, and then determining what pre-processing and/or manipulating of the raw data is required. In this example, the data is again a very simple summary:

name	value
A	-15
B	-20
C	-22
D	-18
E	2
F	6
G	26
H	18

To make our plant data work, we can aggregate the data to look something like the following:

name	value
machine 001	550
machine 002	-200
machine 003	-220
machine 004	800
machine 006	2000

In this particular example, the process to adopt the sample D3 template is even more straightforward:

1. Download the template and save it as an HTML document.
2. Modify the `src=` reference to be a local reference.
3. Add a heading.
4. Change the file name reference.

Once we have completed the preceding steps, we can view our version of the visualization (in a web browser):

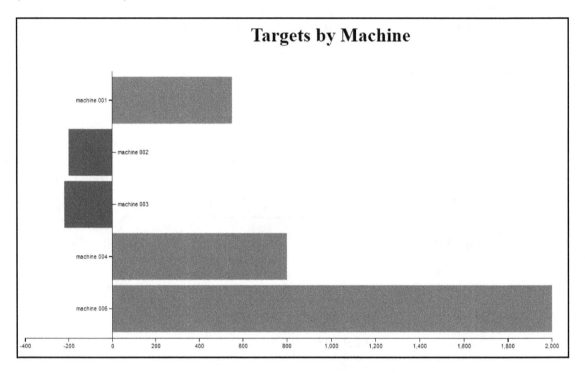

You can see from the visualization generated (shown prior) that **machine 002** and **machine 003** are not hitting the target, while **machine 001**, **machine 004**, and **machine 005** have actually surpassed the target value. The **machine 005** is actually hitting it out of the park by surpassing the target value by 2,000 parts!

One more example

In our final example, let us now look at the D3 **Stacked Area via Nest** template.

This sample template creates a data visualization driven by a summary data file with three fields:

- A key
- A numeric value
- A date (MM/DD/YY)

The following figure shows the data visualization generated by the sample D3 template:

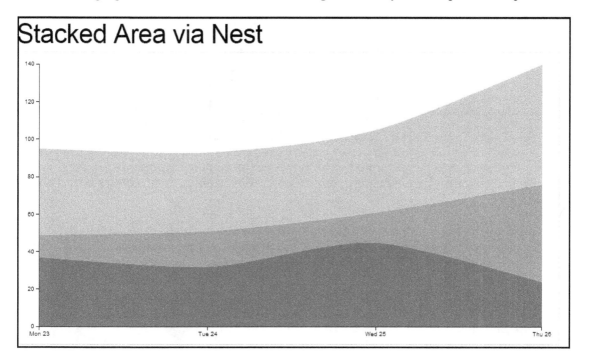

Adopting the sample

As usual, the initial step in adopting any D3 sample template is examining the data source and determining what the similarities might be to a visualization we'd like to create.

In this case, we see a file source with only three fields: a key, a numeric value, and a date:

```
key,value,date
Group1,371,04/23/12
Group2,12,04/23/12
Group3,46,04/23/12
Group1,32,04/24/12
Group2,19,04/24/12
Group3,42,04/24/12
Group1,45,04/25/12
Group2,16,04/25/12
Group3,44,04/25/12
Group1,24,04/26/12
Group2,52,04/26/12
Group3,64,04/26/12
Group1,24,04/27/12
Group2,52,04/27/12
Group3,64,04/27/12
```

Comparing the data to the generated output, we see three values represented in the visualization (Group1, Group2, and Group3) across four dates (**4/23/12**, **4/24/12**, **4/25/12**, and **4/25/12**).

Given that observation, we certainly can imagine a manufacturing plant's need to perhaps visualize the three shifts (shift 1, shift 2, and shift 3) across perhaps a week's worth of days (dates). So, continuing, we can then pre-process our raw plant data into a summarized file of the following fields:

- Date/Time
- Shift ID
- Part count

In this way we can create a new summarized file, such as the following:

```
key,value,date
First,371,04/23/12
Second,12,04/23/12
Third,46,04/23/12
First,32,04/24/12
Second,19,04/24/12
Third,42,04/24/12
First,45,04/25/12
Second,16,04/25/12
Third,44,04/25/12
First,24,04/26/12
Second,52,04/26/12
Third,64,04/26/12
First,24,04/27/12
Second,52,04/27/12
Third,64,04/27/12
```

We should take a few moments at this time to point out that we followed the following thought process when reviewing the templates sample data:

1. The key is grouped and there are three groups. This relates to our three plant shifts.
2. The (numeric) value relates to our (numeric) machine parts count.
3. The date relates to our date–time stamp.

Given these assumptions, we can pre-process or summarize our raw plant data into the appropriate format:

```
key,value,date
First,371,04/23/12
Second,12,04/23/12
Third,46,04/23/12
First,32,04/24/12
Second,19,04/24/12
Third,42,04/24/12
First,45,04/25/12
Second,16,04/25/12
Third,44,04/25/12
First,24,04/26/12
Second,52,04/26/12
Third,64,04/26/12
First,24,04/27/12
Second,52,04/27/12
Third,64,04/27/12
```

We can then generate our visualization:

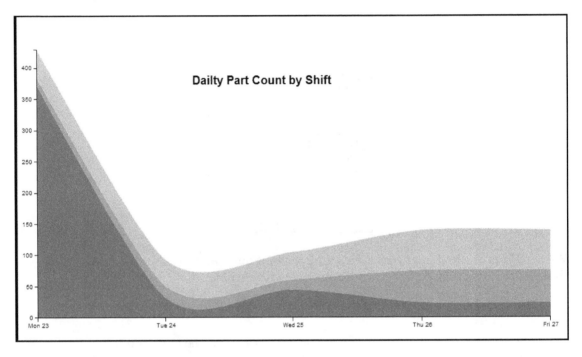

We assume here that by now (after having read through the examples in this chapter) you know that the process to adopt a selected D3 sample template is:

1. Identify the template/example that seems to fit the objectives.
2. Download the template and save it as an HTML document.
3. Make any required HTML document changes (such as `src=` changes, adding a heading, or changing a data file name reference).
4. Pre-process the raw big data into a summarization file formatted to fit the sample D3 requirements.
5. View the document in a web browser.

For those of us so inclined, if you are unable to find a D3 sample that specifically fits your needs, you may endeavor to modify or enhance the existing D3 libraries as needed. That process is beyond the scope of this particular chapter.

In summary, the D3 libraries provide numerous sample templates–freely available for your adoption (to fit your particular data visualization objectives). What we have covered here in this chapter is just a very simple introduction to a small number of those samples.

By following a few simple, easy steps, one can leverage the D3 libraries to generate dynamic visualizations–driven by your big data summations.

The approach has been to adopt and use what is there, but it should be pointed out that since the D3 libraries are opened sourced, one can, if one is so inclined, customize the code to fit any conceivable specific need.

Summary

In this chapter, we covered the idea of visualizing the results of your big data analysis using D3. Simply put, we walked through step by step, the how to of locating and adopting a D3 template to fit the specific needs of your particular big data analysis.

In the next chapter, we will introduce the concept of visual dashboards and how Tableau can be used to create creative, value-add data dashboards.

6
Dashboards for Big Data - Tableau

If a picture is worth a thousand words then a dashboard is worth millions.

Visual dashboards that effectively present the results of multiple analysis–sometimes in real time–are invaluable to businesses of all kinds.

In this chapter, we introduce **Tableau** as a data visualization tool that can be used to construct dashboards, providing working examples demonstrating solutions for effectively presenting results from your big data analysis in a real-time dashboard format.

This chapter is organized into the following main sections:

- About Tableau
- Tableau and big data
- Example 1
- Example 2

About Tableau

A little background around Tableau. Tableau is not free although there are versions free to use (there is a difference) and there is a free use period, after which you must pay for the software.

Tableau offers five main products:

- Tableau Desktop
- Tableau Server
- Tableau Online
- Tableau Reader
- Tableau Public

Tableau Public and Tableau Reader are free to use, while both Tableau Server and Tableau Desktop come with a 14-day fully functional free trial period.

Tableau is also not considered to be open source (as R and D3 are, for example), but Tableau is designed to support how you think, utilizing drag and drop to create visualizations of your data and leverage your natural ability to spot visual patterns quickly.

The foundation of Tableau combines a **Structured Query Language** (**SQL**) for databases with a descriptive language for rendering graphics, to invent a database visualization language called **Visual Query Language** (**VizQL**), making Tableau a unique tool for creating data visualizations.

Another interesting point: Tableau reports over 1,00,000 registered authors who utilize Tableau Public's new Activity feed to keep them up to date by displaying all the recently published data visualizations from Tableau authors around the world.

If you haven't tried Tableau yet, just visit `http://www.tableau.com` and click on the button labeled **Try Tableau for Free** to get started (and as they say, this is a full-version trial. No credit card required!).

Tableau and big data

As I have already stated throughout this book, the idea of plotting millions of data points will never result in a data visualization of much value. In fact, although it is perhaps technically possible to query raw big data directly, it is rarely practical.

We have discussed and (hopefully) established that effective profiling and preprocessing of raw big data is an essential (required) step in any big data visualization process.

Tableau can connect directly to local and cloud data sources, as well as import data for fast in-memory processing and visualization creation. However, just as in the previous chapter, where we explored the rich capabilities provided by the open sourced D3, the correct approach to using Tableau with big data scenarios is to preprocess the raw data source into manageable data files focused on particular objectives.

Although there are many options for data profiling, preprocessing, and manipulation, a tool that is popular with many Tableau users is a product named **Trifacta**, which claims that it is the number-one (data) wrangling solution for Tableau.

> The term **wrangling** is defined loosely as to round up, herd, or otherwise take charge of, and in this case, the wrangling being performed focuses on data.

This chapter is focused on visualizing big data using Tableau, (not particularly the data-preparation step) but based upon Trifacta's popularity within the Tableau community, we'll take a little time here to present an example that works in Trifacta, using the tool to perform some data manipulations (or wrangles, as the Trifacta documentation describes).

> Trifacta can be downloaded for your personal evaluation from www.trifacta.com.

Let's get started.

Example 1 – Sales transactions

In this example, consider global sales transactions being logged by thousands of servers, all day, and every day, twenty-four hours a day. These transaction records contain typical sales information, such as the date the transaction took place (transaction date), a product identifier (product name), the price of the product (SKU price), the total charged (price), the payment type (payment type), and so on.

In addition, the transaction also captures some interesting fields, such as when the user's online account was created, when they last logged on, and so on.

	A	B	C	D	E	F	G	H	I	J	K	L
1	Transaction_date	Product	Price	Payment_	Name	City	State	Country	Account_Created	Last_Login	Latitude	Longitude
2	1/2/2009 6:17	Barbecue Brush	1200	Mastercar	carolina	Basildon	England	United Kin	1/2/2009 6:00	1/2/2009 6:08	51.5	-1.11667
3	1/2/2009 4:53	Barbecue Brush	1200	Visa	Betina	Parkville	MO	United Sta	1/2/2009 4:42	1/2/2009 7:49	39.195	-94.6819
4	1/2/2009 13:08	Barbecue Brush	1200	Mastercar	Federica e Andrea	Astoria	OR	United Sta	1/1/2009 16:21	1/3/2009 12:32	46.18806	-123.83
5	1/3/2009 14:44	Barbecue Brush	1200	Visa	Gouya	Echuca	Victoria	Australia	9/25/2005 21:13	1/3/2009 14:22	-36.1333	144.75
6	1/4/2009 12:56	Grille Rack	3600	Visa	Gerd W	Cahaba He	AL	United Sta	11/15/2008 15:47	1/4/2009 12:45	33.52056	-86.8025
7	1/4/2009 13:19	Barbecue Brush	1200	Visa	LAURENCE	Mickleton	NJ	United Sta	9/24/2008 15:19	1/4/2009 13:04	39.79	-75.2381

Adding more context

Many times there is a desire to view transactional data within a particular context—a context that is based on a secondary data source. For example, suppose that there is data available to us that contains promotional marketing information: a file extracted from a database containing the sales and marketing efforts for the products in our sales transactional file.

This information may list the following:

- **Promotion_Name**: This is the name the marketing team uses to refer to the effort
- **Promotion_Start_Date**: This is the date and time the particular effort was launched
- **Promotion_End_Date**: This is the date and time the particular effort was completed (blank if the campaign is still in progress)
- **Promotion_Duration** (in days): This is the number of days elapsed from the start of the promotion until completion or, to date
- **Promotion_Type**: This is the type of promotion used, such as social media, television, radio, Internet, print, and so on
- **Promotion_Budget**: This is the dollar amount budgeted for the promotion
- **Promotion_Spent**: This is the dollar amount spent on the promotion to date

With the preceding data in mind, we'll use Trifacta to accomplish the following.

Let's say that, through profiling, we've discovered that there are some glitches with the supplied promotion data. Since this information is a manually maintained record of marketing promotions, we find that there may be duplicate records (the same promotion listed more than once), missing values (for example, the value for the **Promotion_Spent** field is sometimes blank), and finally, the **Promotion_Type** field contains only numeric values (a reference number indicating the type of the promotion, rather than its descriptive name).

We should point out that we've skipped over the profiling step here in this example since we covered data profiling techniques in Chapter 3, *Understanding Your Data Using R,* but we could have used Trifacta to profile our data and identify the aforementioned issues. The reader is encouraged to investigate Trifacta's profiling features.

Wrangling the data

The first step in using Trifacta to address the issues identified with our promotion data is to create a project within Trifacta. From the Trifacta workspace (or desktop), which is shown in the following screenshot, click on the button labeled **Create**, and then select **Create Project**:

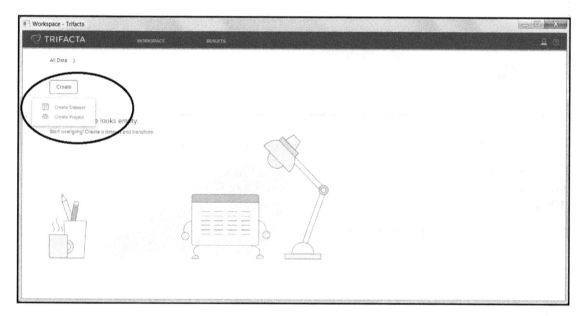

From there you can add a name for your project and a brief description:

Then, in (about) the center left of the screen, click on the link that says **create new dataset**.

Next, on the **Create Dataset** screen, you can click on the icon in the upper left that is labeled **Add File**. Trifacta then provides the opportunity to **Drag & drop** or Windows browse to (**Choose File**):

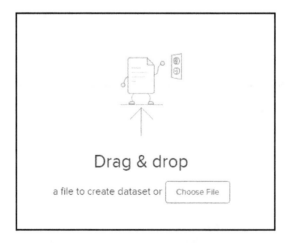

Once we've added our promotion file, Trifacta displays some initial statistics (its size) and allows us to add the file to our project by clicking the bright blue button in the lower right of the screen (labeled **Add to Project**):

Back on the project screen we can now click **Save Project** (saving the change we made to our Trifacta project, of adding the file). On the main workspace, Trifacta shows us our project (**MyBookSample**) and our file (**global promotions performance raw duplicate records**):

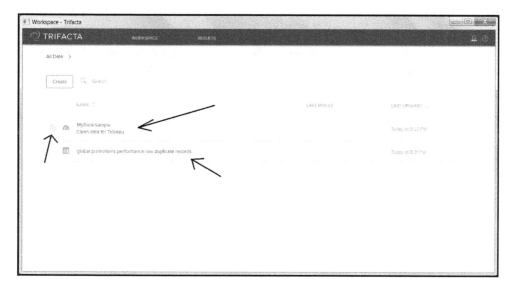

Notice, to the left of our project name, the **clock** icon. If we click on that icon, the **Transform** button is displayed next to our file:

Once you click on **Transform**, Trifacta reads through and studies the file.

The results of the study are shown on the **Transformer** page (shown in the following screenshot), where you can identify any data that you want to transform, and build transformation scripts to perform the desired transformations.

When you create or change a script, those changes are immediately applied to the data shown, so that you can preview the results in real time and quickly iterate through the process of tweaking your script to meet your requirements:

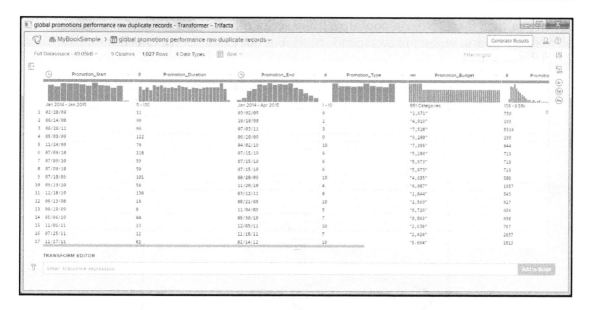

In our example, we know that there are 1,027 records in our promotion file and suspect that the file may contain duplicate records. We'll address that concern first. To do this, Trifacta makes it super easy with the `deduplicate` command.

 Through the Trifacta Script panel, you can evaluate and modify scripts that you create. On the **Transformer** page, the script is represented as a series of icons on the right-hand side of the screen.

To add the `deduplicate` command to our script, you can simply click on the **Transform Editor** (shown in the following screenshot) at the bottom left of the transformation or **Transformer** page:

When you click there, Trifacta pops up a list of script commands to select from (you can also type free form typescript commands here). For our example, we can click on `deduplicate` (adding the command to our script):

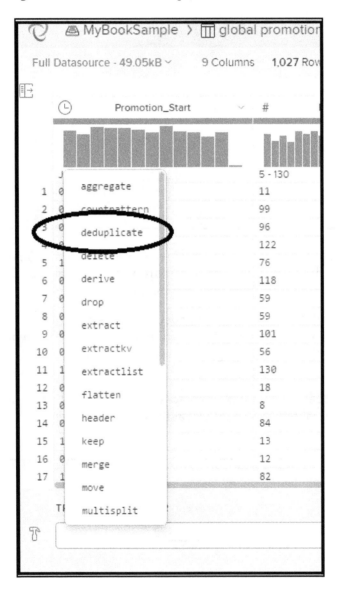

After we add the `deduplicate` command (to our script) we can click on the **script** icon (circled in the following screenshot) and the script will appear.

Notice that there are three rows or lines of the script already present (**splitrows, split**, and **header**). These have been added for us by Trifacta since our file is a **CSV** formatted file. The last line of the script shows the `deduplicate` command that we just added (underlined in the following screenshot).

Having reviewed the script, we can then click on the **Generate Results** button located in the upper right of the **Transformer** page (see the arrow in the following screenshot):

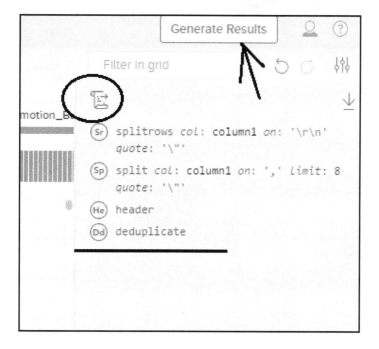

Trifacta then asks us what format to generate the results in **CSV**, **JSON**, or **TDE** (are supported) and if we want the output compressed:

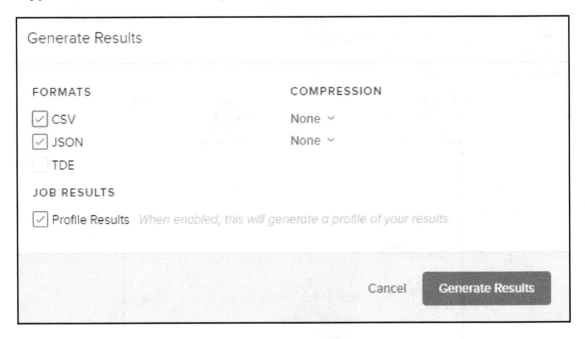

I left the default selections and clicked **Generate Results** (again).

After Trifacta executes the script, you are returned to your project results page where the summary space is shown (the top of the following screenshot). Clicking on the button labeled **Summary** shows us the **Results Summary** details.

Note that the record count (**Rows**) of our updated file is **1,026**. You may recall that originally, our file record count was 1,027, so Trifacta performed the dedup and removed one record. It's really that easy!

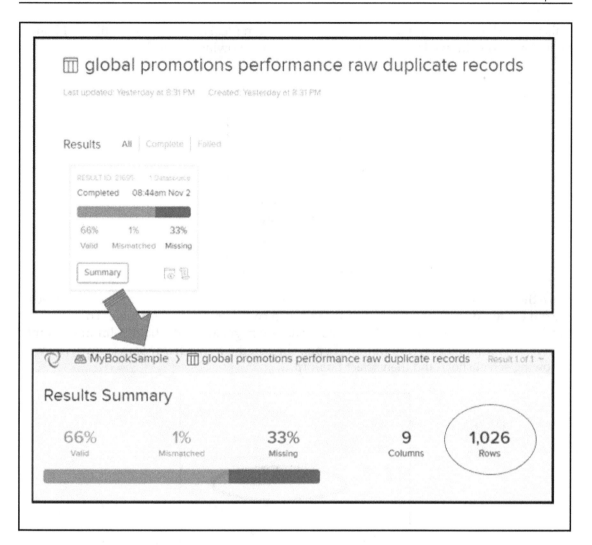

So now we've seen that one can easily and effortlessly identify and drop duplicate records from a file with the help of Trifacta. Another task Trifacta makes easy work of is performing lookups, such as replacing a numeric identifier (such as the promotion type ID in our file) with a more user-friendly description or name.

This is done by simply providing Trifacta a conversion file. Here, a two-field file (field one is the **key** and field two is the **value**) is shown in the following screenshot:

1	Social media
2	Television
3	Radio
4	Print
5	Internet
6	Direct Mail
7	Telephone
8	Combinational
9	Give-a-way
10	Contest

Once the file is uploaded to Trifacta, we can add it to our project (following the same steps we did earlier to add our promotion file) and then configure the lookup logic. To accomplish this, we will start at the **Transformation** page, locate the field/column we want to perform the lookup on (**Promotion_Type**), click on the **down arrow** icon (shown in the following screenshot), and then select **Lookup...**.

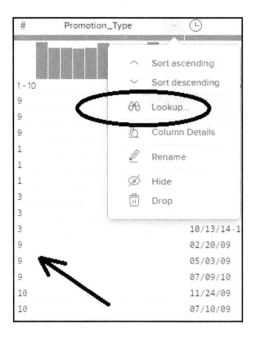

Once you select **Lookup...**, the **Select Dataset** screen is presented (shown in the following screenshot) where you can select the lookup file and click on the button labeled **Select**:

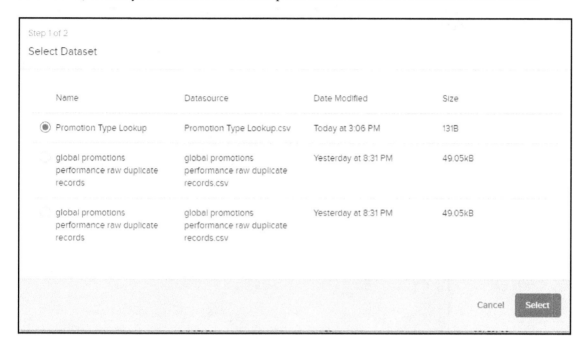

Next, we need to select our lookup key and then click on the button labeled **Execute Lookup**:

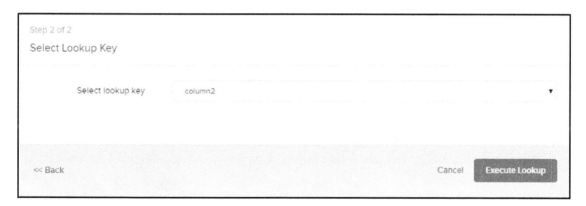

Upon clicking this button, Trifacta adds the commands that are necessary to perform the lookup to the script and then runs the script immediately. The following is the result showing the addition of a new field, **column3**, which now holds the converted value (the **Promotion_Type** description):

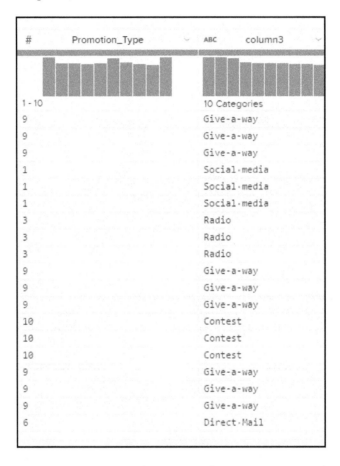

 You probably want to use the rename feature to rename the default **column3** to something more descriptive!

The final issue with our data is missing values. From our profiling, we've learned that some records within our promotion file are missing a value for the **Promotion_Budget_Burn** field. Again, you will find that Trifacta makes this problem easy to resolve.

Since we already have our file loaded and added to our project, we can go to the **Transformer** page and navigate to the **Promotion_Budget_Burnt** field. Trifacta indicates that there are missing values by showing a gray colored section in the field heading's quality bar. If you hover your mouse pointer over the area, Trifacta informs us that there are two records with missing values (in this field):

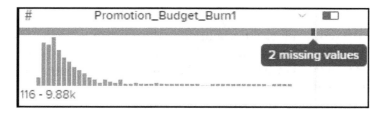

To resolve this, you can click on the gray section known as the **SUGGESTIONS** card. Trifacta automatically generates a series of suggested transforms that you can apply to the missing data. These **SUGGESTIONS** are displayed across the bottom of the page:

By default, Trifacta replaces missing values with a null value, but you can change that by clicking on the suggestion box of the transform logic that you think best fits your needs (**Keep**, **Delete**, **Set**, or **Derive**), and then click on the button labeled **Modify**:

This opens the **TRANSFORM EDITOR** where you can change the script presented. I have selected **set** (shown in the following screenshot):

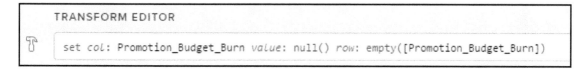

TRANSFORM EDITOR

```
set col: Promotion_Budget_Burn value: null() row: empty([Promotion_Budget_Burn])
```

I have also changed the value (to have the missing values set to):

TRANSFORM EDITOR

set *col*: Promotion_Budget_Burn *value*: 99999 *row*: empty([Promotion_Budget_Burn])

After you change the script value, Trifacta updates the preview with the results of your transformation. The replacement values will be highlighted in green. When you are satisfied with your data transformation, click **Add to Script**, and then click on **Generate Results** to save the updated file.

Moving on

Hopefully, at this point, we have ignited the reader's interest in Trifacta. Although we have only touched on a very few of the many features offered by the tool, one can see that it has enormous potential for wrangling your data!

Now let's move on to visualizing our data with Tableau:

A Tableau dashboard

Back to our original visualization objective! Remember that we want to be able to create a visual dashboard showing total sales dollars for each product by period. In addition, we also want to overlay the promotion information we have been provided with to compare the effect of various promotional efforts on sales.

We'll again assume here that we've previously completed profiling the data, and so we have an understanding of its content and have established context. We also know that using the promotion data, we want to review our sales in a different context (for example, as affected by our organizations marketing efforts).

To that point, as with the examples throughout this book, our big data (the sales transactions) needs to be aggregated into a format (or formats) that we can use for visualization.

Earlier in this chapter, we investigated Trifacta, but again, I'll point out that you as the data scientist have the ability to select from a large number of viable technologies. We'll assume that while using your favorite tool (whatever that is) you have successfully aggregated the data and are ready to exploit Tableau to create a visual dashboard.

Based upon our initial interest (product sales over time) we've created an aggregated or summarized file consisting of the product name and a total sales dollar sales figure for each month.

The file format is a comma separated file (or **CSV**) partially shown in the following screenshot:

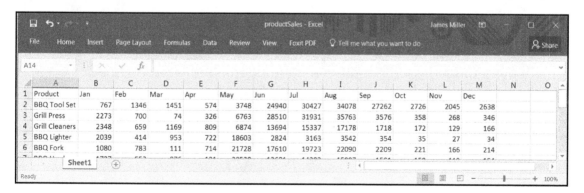

Product	Jan	Feb	Mar	Apr	May	Jun	Jul	Aug	Sep	Oct	Nov	Dec
BBQ Tool Set	767	1346	1451	574	3748	24940	30427	34078	27262	2726	2045	2638
Grill Press	2273	700	74	326	6763	28510	31931	35763	3576	358	268	346
Grill Cleaners	2348	659	1169	809	6874	13694	15337	17178	1718	172	129	166
BBQ Lighter	2039	414	953	722	18603	2824	3163	3542	354	35	27	34
BBQ Fork	1080	783	111	714	21728	17610	19723	22090	2209	221	166	214

Our second summarized file is the promotion data and it is in a similar format of **Promotion type** and a total budget burn figure for each month. That file is also a **CSV** formatted file (and partially shown in the following screenshot):

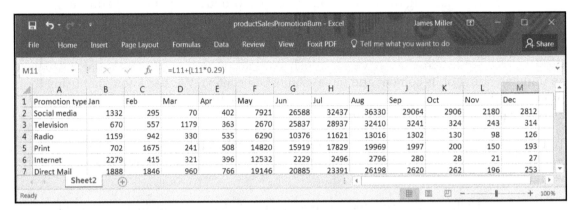

	A	B	C	D	E	F	G	H	I	J	K	L	M
1	Promotion type	Jan	Feb	Mar	Apr	May	Jun	Jul	Aug	Sep	Oct	Nov	Dec
2	Social media	1332	295	70	402	7921	26588	32437	36330	29064	2906	2180	2812
3	Television	670	557	1179	363	2670	25837	28937	32410	3241	324	243	314
4	Radio	1159	942	330	535	6290	10376	11621	13016	1302	130	98	126
5	Print	702	1675	241	508	14820	15919	17829	19969	1997	200	150	193
6	Internet	2279	415	321	396	12532	2229	2496	2796	280	28	21	27
7	Direct Mail	1888	1846	960	766	19146	20885	23391	26198	2620	262	196	253

Now that we have our summary files, we can start consuming them with Tableau.

We get started by opening Tableau's start page (by default, Tableau opens to the start page). The Tableau start page is a central location from which you can **Connect** (to data), **Open** (existing workbooks), and **Discover** (content created by the Tableau community).

On the start page (shown in the following screenshot), under **Connect**, click **Excel** (note: the **Connect** pane lists the different types of data you can connect to; our summary files were saved as **CSV** files then opened in MS Excel, reviewed, and saved as a worksheet). Next, at the **Open** dialog box, we can navigate to our summary files and open them (we'll select the promotion burn file first):

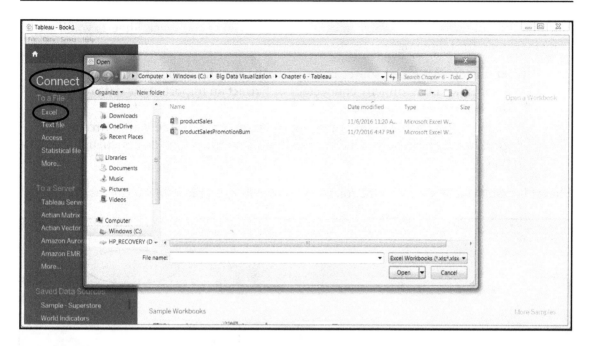

After connecting to the data, the data source page will show whatever worksheets that it found in your data:

Once we drag our sheet to the Tableau canvas (we only have one sheet, **Sheet1**) you'll see that you can do the following:

1. At the top of the data source page, you can select how you want to connect to the data, either **Live** (directly connected) or **Extract** an import of the data (or subset of the data, saved within Tableau).

2. At the bottom of the data source page, you can preview the data source in the grid. In the grid, you can hide or rename a column in the data, or change the data type.

Sheet1 is displayed as shown in the following screenshot, on the Tableau canvas:

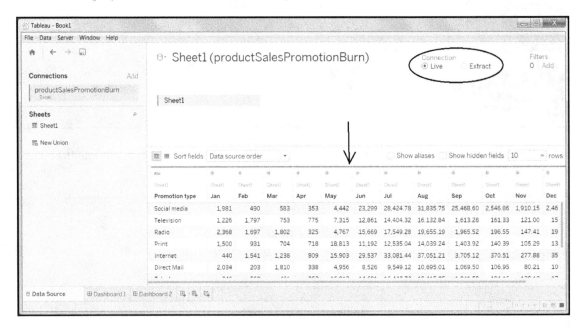

Next, we click the new sheet tab to go to the new worksheet so we can begin experimenting with the data and build the visualization or the view (of our data) that we want:

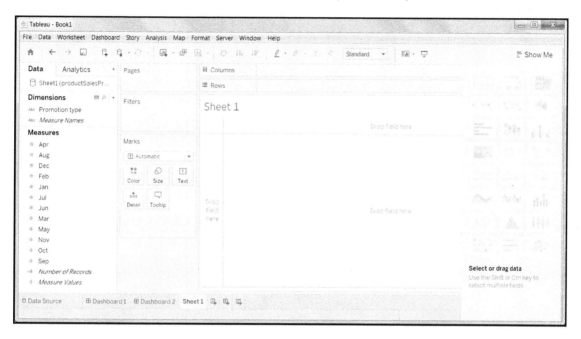

First, we'll create a basic view of the month-by-month promotion spend (or burn) then we can expand that view to include more data, filter the view to drill into the most important data, and finally, to add color to make the results stand out.

On the left-hand side of the worksheet is the **Data** pane (shown in the following screenshot). The Tableau **Data** pane contains a variety of different kinds of fields, including **Dimensions** and **Measures**. The columns from our file are shown here as fields:

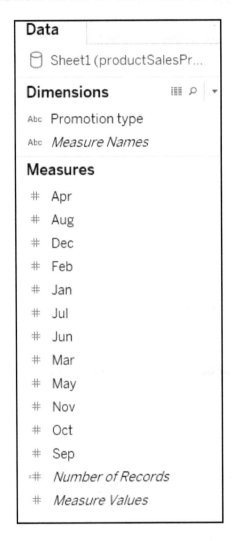

You'll notice that dimensions typically hold categorical data (our **Promotion type**), while measures hold numeric data (such as our promotion burn dollar totals).

When you build a view, you add the desired fields from the **Data** pane. You can do this in different ways, but let's drag our fields from the **Data** pane and drop them onto the **Columns** and **Rows** that are visible across the top of the Tableau worksheet:

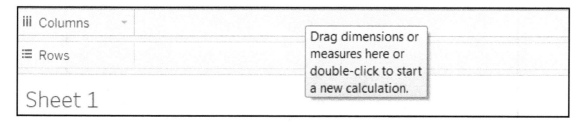

I added **Promotion type** as columns and **Measure Values** (the monthly promotion burn total) as rows (note: the **Columns** and **Rows** are referred to as the columns shelf and the rows shelf).

Tableau immediately creates the visualization shown in the following screenshot:

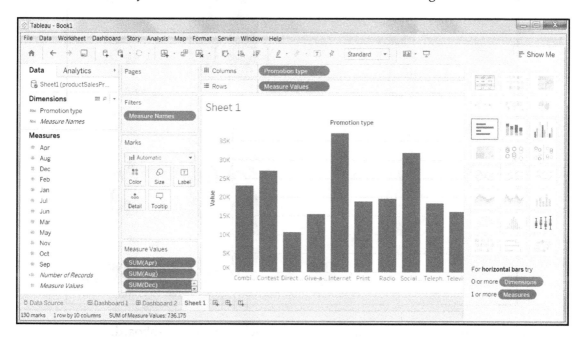

The preceding visualization provides insight on the spend by promotion type.

If we switch the columns/rows selections, putting **Measure Names** (the names of the months) as the columns and **Measure Values** (again, the promotion burn or spend) as the rows, we can see the total spent each month on promotions:

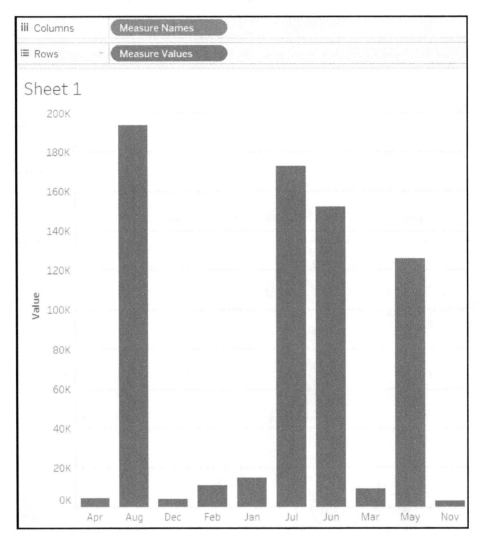

This is more in line with what we have in mind to include in our dashboard.

If we repeat the preceding steps (adding our product sales data to Tableau and visualizing that data) we get the following:

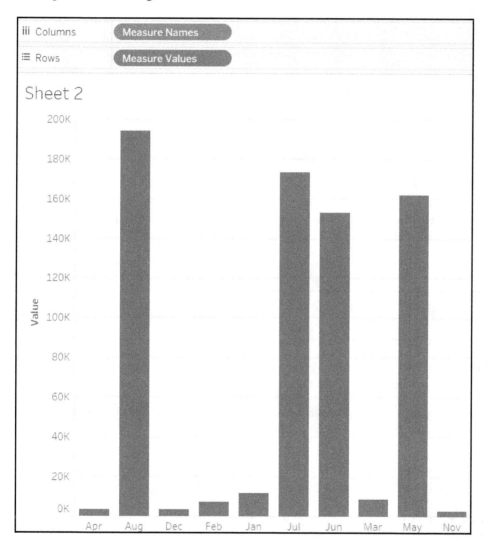

So, now we have two (albeit very simple) views of our data and we should save them in a Tableau workbook. Once we save our views, we can use them to construct a dashboard. In addition, we could share the individually saved workbooks with other users, either by sending the file or publishing the workbook to the Web.

Saving the workbook

Standard MS Windows commands work in Tableau; for example, *Ctrl + S* on your keyboard will save your work.

You can browse to a file location to save the workbook, or go with the default, letting Tableau save the workbook in the `Workbooks` folder in the **My Tableau Repository**.

As always, it's a good idea to rename any work you do with an appropriate name or identifier. In this case, just like you would do in MS Excel, you can right-click on each Tableau worksheet tab and specify a filename for the workbook.

I renamed our sheets as **Promotion Spend** and **Product Sales**:

Another bit of information: when you save your work, you can specify a file type. The file type options are as follows:

- Tableau workbook (`.twb`): Saves all the sheets and their connection information in a workbook file–but the data is not included
- Tableau packaged workbook (`.twbx`): Saves all the sheets, their connection information, and any local resources (for example, local file data sources, background images, custom geocoding, and so on)

Now that we have our views saved in a workbook, we can proceed to build a Tableau dashboard!

Presenting our work

As per Tableau product documentation:

> *"The ideal visualization combines science with art. With formatting, dashboards, and stories you can make your data discoveries clearer, more persuasive, and beautiful."*

A **dashboard** is a collection (of worksheets and supporting information) shown in a single place, so you can compare and monitor simultaneously rather than having to click through individual worksheets. Similar to worksheets, dashboards update with the most recent data from their data source. That means when you modify the worksheet, the dashboard it is part of is updated and when you modify the view in the dashboard, the worksheet is updated.

You create a dashboard similar to how we created our worksheet. After you click the **New Dashboard** icon (at the bottom of the workbook) you can click the views we built (listed under **Sheets** on the left) and drag them onto the dashboard sheet on the right:

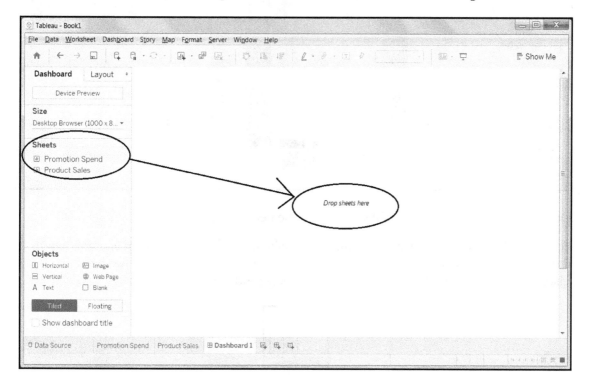

In addition to adding our views to the dashboard, you can add web pages, images, text, blank space, and layout containers (more on this later).

The following is our simple dashboard providing a comparison between monthly **Promotional Spend** and monthly **Product Sales**:

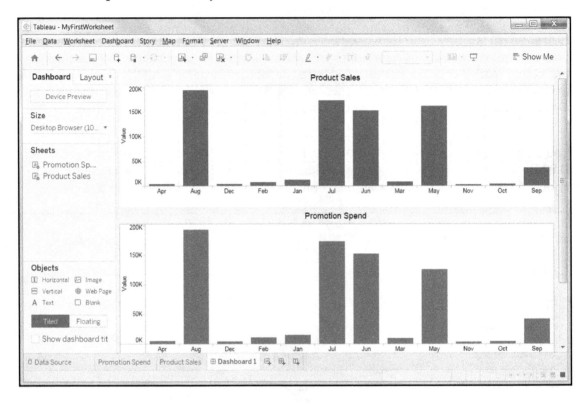

Once you have a dashboard, Tableau offers some neat tricks.

For example, if you select a sheet within the dashboard and click the **Swap** icon (shown in the following screenshot) or *Ctrl – W* (the shortcut for swap) you can flip the sheets visualization from a vertical to a horizontal display (and back):

If you move your mouse over the upper left of a sheet, you can click on **Go to Sheet**, which loads the sheet view so you can review and refine it. For instance, in our example, using drag and drop, I placed the month names in calendar order and changed the color of the **Promotion Spend** visualization to green (there are various ways to accomplish these refinement tasks; this is just one method).

More tools

Tableau has numerous tools that can be used to refine and (hopefully) improve your visualizations, such as: re-coloring, resizing, adding or changing labels, changing the type of visualization, adding calculation formulas, and so on. Tableau always applies these changes in real time, so you can observe the effects before saving the change:

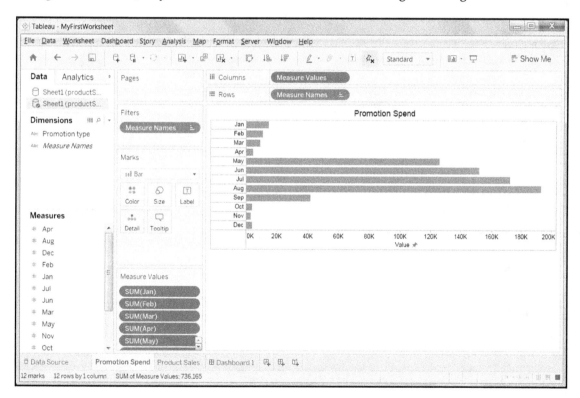

Another feature Tableau provides is filtering. If you right-click on a visualization's border, you can select **Filters**, and then **Measure Names**:

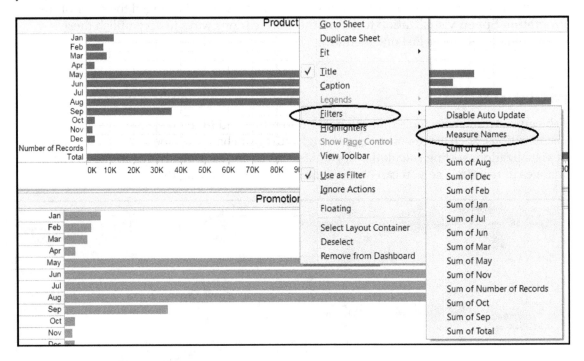

This offers the user the ability to interact with the data, exploring what data the visualization is based upon:

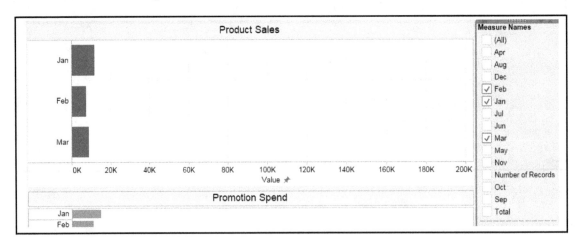

Yet another useful feature is the ability to add calculations directly to a visualization. If you click on the menu labeled **Analysis**, and then **Create Calculated Field...**, Tableau presents a dialog where you can write impromptu formulas to add to your visualizations (without having to add them to the original data file):

The following is our dashboard showing our visualizations a little more refined.

We might note that perhaps our promotional spend isn't really working as expected; in other words, how do the resulting product sales compare to the **Promotion Spend**?

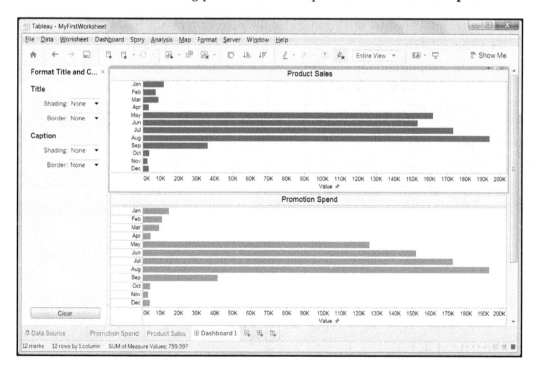

Let's see if we can further refine our dashboard a bit more and increase its value to the business.

Example 2

Using the previous business scenario (of **Product Sales** and **Promotion Spend** totals) as a starting point, let's build a dashboard that might be more real world in nature.

What's the goal? – purpose and audience

The very first step in creating any dashboard, using any tool or even manually, is establishing an objective, or what is the dashboard trying to solve?

Let's consider the idea that the marketing executives of our organization BIGGIG Enterprises want to monitor how their **Promotion Spend** might be affecting overall **Product Sales**.

Our dashboard requirements might be listed as follows:

- Show total product sales dollars for the current year–**CY Sales**
- Show total product sales dollars for the prior year–**PY Sales**
- Show total promotion spend dollars for the current year
- Show total product spend dollars for the prior year
- Visualize monthly product sales dollars with an *average* indicator
- Visualize monthly promotional spend dollars with an *average* indicator
- Visualize sales versus spend by month
- Visualize the trend of promotional spend as a percent of total product sales
- Since this dashboard's target audience is to be C-level executives, it needs to utilize an attractive and useful design

The following is our **Promotion Spend Effect on Sales** executive dashboard:

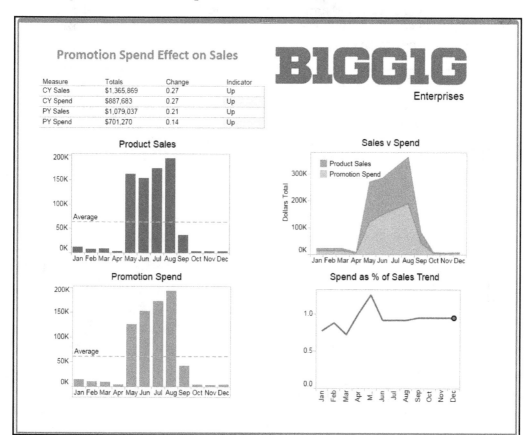

Let us now walk through the steps that are significant in creating our dashboard using Tableau.

The easy work first—headings and logos. There are several container objects available to be added to your dashboard. These include **Horizontal** and **Vertical** layout containers, **Text**, **Image**, **Web Page**, and **Blank**.

To add a heading to our dashboard, you can click on the **Text** object (in the objects tile shown in the preceding screenshot) and drag it onto the dashboard. The **Edit Text** dialog is then presented. Here you can type the heading and set alignment, font style, size, and color (shown in the following screenshot):

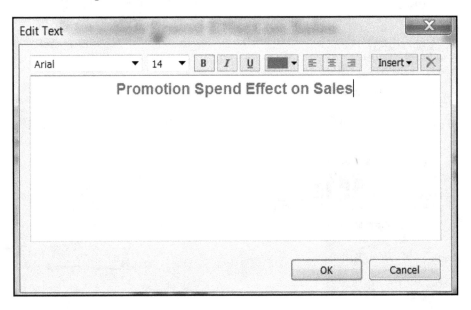

That's pretty easy. The steps to add a logo are similar–just click and drag the **Image** object to the dashboard. This gives you the opportunity to browse to and select an image file to be used in your dashboard.

Sales and spend

We created the **Product Sales** and **Promotion Spend** visualizations (or views) earlier in this chapter. Since changes to worksheets are immediately applied to any dashboard they are included in, we can reopen those worksheets, make modifications, and then add them to our new dashboard.

The only changes made to these views were to remove the axis title and add a reference line. To remove the **Value** title from the axis, you can right-click on the axis and select **Edit Access...**, and then clear the text from the **Titles** section of the **Edit Axis** dialog.

To add the **Average** reference line to these visualizations, you can right-click on the dollar's axis in the worksheets and then select **Add Reference Line**. In the **Add Reference Line, Band, or Box** dialog box (shown in the following screenshot), select **Line**:

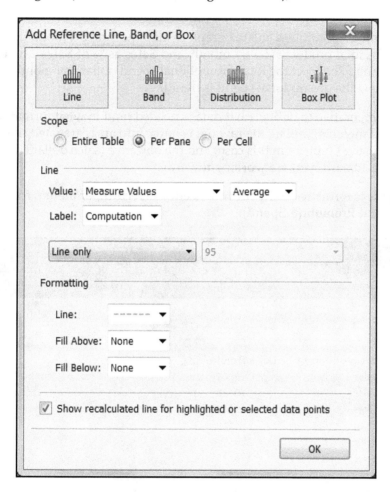

 I've also selected **Per Pane** (as the scope), **Measure Values** and **Average** (for line), and tweaked the formatting as shown (the reader can review and experiment with these settings as desired).

Sales v Spend and Spend as % of Sales Trend

To make our dashboard more valuable, we've added two additional visualizations (or views of data).

The **Sales v Spend** graph utilizes an area graph to map the total promotional spend by month against the total product sales by month, and **Sales as % of Sales Trend**, which utilizes a line graph to connect the total promotional spend dollars by month into a line to give a sense of how the promotional spend is trending.

As always, it is imperative to define what data is needed (and in what format) for your visualization and then manipulate the raw data source into an aggregated file suitable for the tool you are using (Tableau in this case) and the objective (sales dollars' versus spend dollars, in our dashboard) you are working towards.

The following file is formatted to fit our first need: one record per month, for each measure (**Product Sales** and **Promotion Spend**):

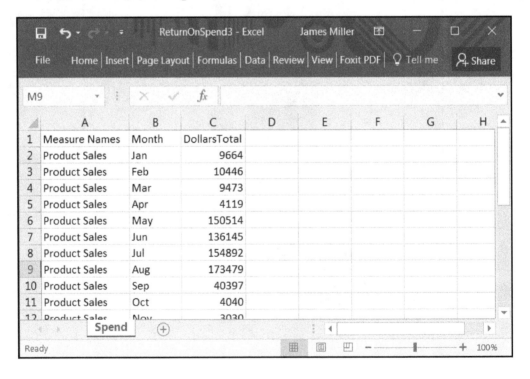

Once we add this file as a new data source (from the menu **Data**, **New Data Source**, **Excel**, and so on), we can create a new worksheet, defining our visualization (the desired view of the data). In this worksheet, we use the month names as the columns and the dollar amounts as the rows.

 Based upon the format of the data (in this example there are two distinct measures), Tableau maps them for us (Tableau will map or plot every distinct measure in the file for us).

The following is our **Sales v Spend** visualization:

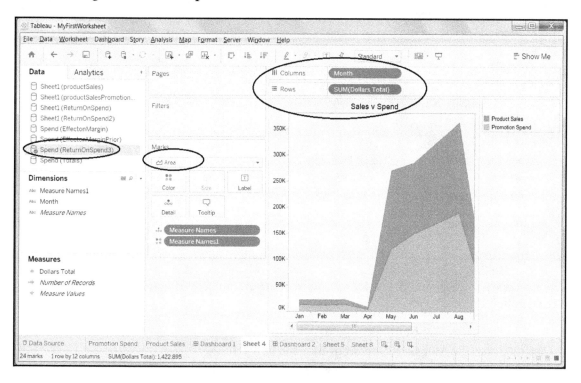

Moving on, the easiest method to visualize the promotion spend dollars as a percentage of sales dollars was to add a calculated field to our aggregated file (yes, you can add complex, calculated formal fields within Tableau–which we will see later in this chapter–but for now, I've decided to add the data to the data source file).

As shown in the following screenshot, I've added the new **Percent of Sales** field (and then set up the file as a new data source in Tableau):

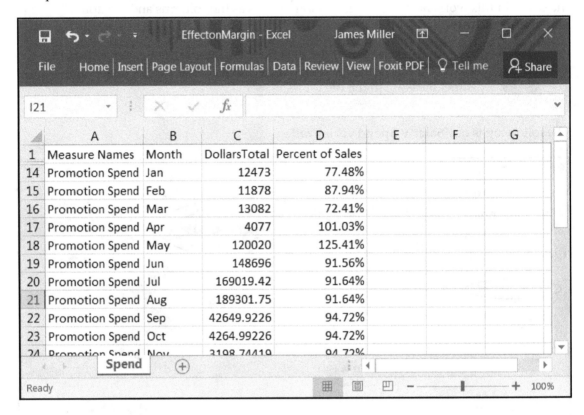

	A	B	C	D	E	F	G
1	Measure Names	Month	DollarsTotal	Percent of Sales			
14	Promotion Spend	Jan	12473	77.48%			
15	Promotion Spend	Feb	11878	87.94%			
16	Promotion Spend	Mar	13082	72.41%			
17	Promotion Spend	Apr	4077	101.03%			
18	Promotion Spend	May	120020	125.41%			
19	Promotion Spend	Jun	148696	91.56%			
20	Promotion Spend	Jul	169019.42	91.64%			
21	Promotion Spend	Aug	189301.75	91.64%			
22	Promotion Spend	Sep	42649.9226	94.72%			
23	Promotion Spend	Oct	4264.99226	94.72%			
24	Promotion Spend	Nov	3198.744419	94.72%			

Once again, we create a new worksheet, select the new file from the **Data** list, and create the visualization or view:

1. Drag the **Month** dimension, to columns.
2. Drag the **Measure Percent of Sales** to rows.
3. Select **Line** as the visualization type.
4. Edit the **Title** and **Axis** text.
5. Save the worksheet.

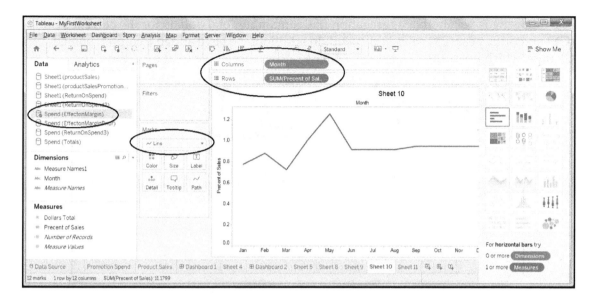

Tables and indicators

The last puzzle piece of our dashboard is the text table in the upper left of the screen:

Measure	Totals	Change	Indicator
CY Sales	$1,365,869	0.27	Up
CY Spend	$887,683	0.27	Up
PY Sales	$1,079,037	0.21	Up
PY Spend	$701,270	0.14	Up

In Tableau, you can create text tables (also called cross-tabs or pivot tables) by placing one dimension on rows and another dimension on columns. You then complete the view by dragging one or more measures to the **Text on the Marks** card.

The following is yet another aggregation file, containing total dollars for the **current year** (**CY**) and **prior year** (**PY**) sales and spend. In addition, we have added a column named **Change**, which holds the percentage increase or decrease of the total from the prior year.

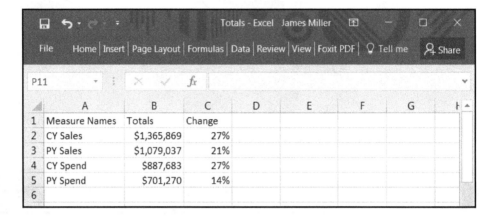

In the following screenshot, we see the file after it has been added as a Tableau data source:

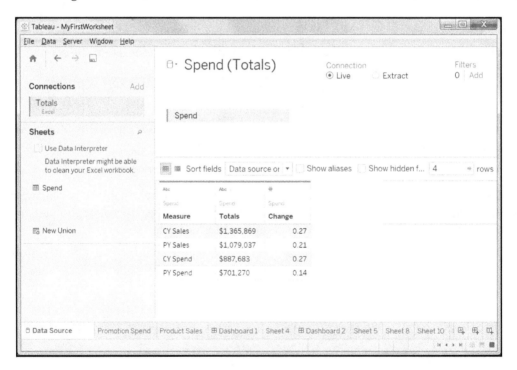

After we have added our new data source, we can proceed to create a new worksheet (shown in the following screenshot):

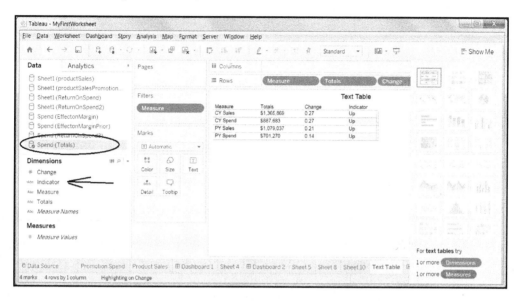

You may notice that we've added yet another new column, a Tableau calculated field named **Indicator**. A calculated field is one that you create by using a Tableau formula to modify the existing fields in your data source. These fields are then saved as part of your data source:

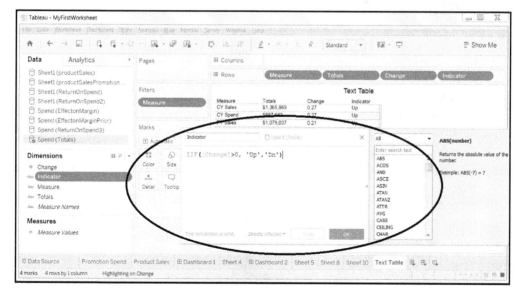

You use the calculation editor (shown in the following screenshot) to create these fields. To open the Tableau calculation editor, you can click the dropdown to the right of **Dimensions** in the **Data** pane and choose **Create Calculated Field**:

The preceding screenshot shows the opened calculation editor showing how I have created a logical calculated field. The formula indicates that if the value of the current cell in the **Change** column is positive (greater than zero) then it's **Up** from the prior year (otherwise it is **Dn** from the prior year). The calculation editor automatically checks the formulas syntax and (in the lower left) displays **The calculation is valid**. There are many types of calculated fields; logical is just one example.

All together now

Now that we've constructed each of our dashboards components–in the form of static text (the dashboard heading), a logo (the image file), and our five individual views, all that is left is to assemble the actual dashboard:

1. As discussed earlier in this chapter, creating a new dashboard starts with clicking the **New Dashboard** icon at the bottom of the Tableau workbook. Our new dashboard tab will appear on the left and lists the sheets in your workbook.
2. Once you have created the new dashboard, you can click the views we built (listed under **Sheets** on the left) and drag them to our dashboard sheet on the right.
3. In addition to adding views to your dashboard, you can add objects, including web pages, images, text, blank space, and layout containers. To add our objects, select an item under **Objects** on the left and drag it to the dashboard sheet.

Layout containers are very useful for fine-tuning how your dashboard resizes itself when users interact with it. In this example, rather than leveraging the horizontal or vertical layout container objects, I've elected to just use the floating approach, and manually move and place my components in the dashboard.

After you've built a dashboard, Tableau gives you the ability to create layouts to support specific devices so that people who interact with it experience a dashboard specifically designed for that device (a phone, tablet, desktop, specific browser, and so on). Using Tableaus device preview feature, you can open your dashboard and see what it will look like on the particular selected device.

Summary

In this chapter, we started by introducing Trifacta Wrangler as a means to profile and manipulate your raw big data into a format that can be easily consumed and visualized. In addition, we explored the concept of using a secondary data source to provide context to a primary data source.

Next, we presented Tableau as a tool to consume prepared data and create valuable visualizations as individual components of interactive dashboards.

In the next chapter, we will cover outliers and provide working example solutions to deal with outliers and other data anomalies using Python.

7
Dealing with Outliers Using Python

A certain percentage of all data will consist of what is referred to as outliers–those points or responses beyond reasonable ranges established for the data, based upon its context. General responses to found outliers become increasingly challenging within big data initiatives.

In this chapter, we will focus on the topic of dealing with outliers as they relate to big data visualization, introduce the Python language, and offer working examples demonstrating solutions for effectively dealing with data outliers and other anomalies in big data, using Python.

This chapter is organized into the following main sections:

- About Python
- Python and big data
- Outliers
- Some basic examples
- More examples

About Python

Python became available sometime during the late 1980s and bargains to be a very easy to comprehend scripting language. It shines at tasks such as integration, has all sorts of ready-made tools, and can connect to databases and other systems.

Python is also very popular in web development, though primarily on the backend side, and since Python runs interactively or in live mode, it is difficult to pack up a Python solution into a single executable file for distribution.

Furthermore, Python is not a desktop application but it is a scripting language that is designed by emphasizing code readability, and its syntax allows programmers to (perhaps) solve problems in fewer lines of code (than in languages such as C++ or Java) and without all the overhead.

The reader should note that there are various free versions of downloadable Python IDEs such as **Wingware** (available at `www.wingware.com`) that make scripting with Python very manageable (and even enjoyable!):

The bottom line? Python is very versatile and powerful and it has increased in popularity over the last several years and it is unquestionably a valid choice for your big data projects.

Python and big data

Python is a very good choice for big data manipulations and, as we'll see in this chapter, for addressing big data outliers. This is due to the following points:

- It's easy to understand and use. You can learn Python relatively quickly and get on to the true task at hand: manipulating and processing your big data.
- Python comes with a wide range of prebuilt libraries focused on data processing, visualization, and other data manipulations. This saves, even more, Python is very versatile and powerful and has increased in popularity of thetime by providing solutions to the most fundamental tasks required to process big data.
- Although Python is a general purpose language that runs just about anywhere, it is flexible and nimble enough to provide the ability to create very custom solutions to address unique problems associated with big data.

All the preceding features prove the point for using Python for manipulating and processing big data to generate quick insights valuable to organizations. Python is a powerful tool to get this value instantly and remain competitive in the marketplace.

Let's get started.

Outliers

In this chapter, we want to deal with the manipulation of big data sources to address data outliers. So let's have a quick reminder for the reader:

Outliers can be defined as:

- A data point that is way out of keeping with the others
- That piece of data that doesn't fit
- Either a very high value or a very low value
- Unusual observations within the data
- An observation point that is distant from all others

Options for outliers

The options that are generally accepted for dealing with found outliers in big data are:

- **Delete**: This includes the outlier values or even the actual variable where the outliers exist
- **Transform**: This includes the values or the variable itself

Delete

If you have just a few outliers, you may decide to simply delete those outlying values (they then become blank or missing values, which usually are easier to deal with in a visualization). Also, if the variable just doesn't make sense, or if there are just too many outliers in that variable (or maybe you just don't need the variable), you can just delete the entire variable.

Transform

Other than deleting, you also have the option of transforming. This is a bit more involved; however, generally, the idea is that you can change the outlier value to the next highest/lowest (non-outlier) number or change the value to the next highest/lowest (non-outlier) number plus one unit increment higher/lower or change the value based upon some other logic reasonable to your objective.

Finally, you can also transform the variable itself. This involves understanding the variables non-normality and then using appropriate logic and formulas to change the variable. The simple examples use the `mean` or `sum` computations.

Outliers identified

The notion of identifying outliers may be referred to using different names; such as:

- Outlier mining
- Outlier modeling
- Novelty detection
- Anomaly detection

This chapter's perspective on outliers is addressing them, not identifying them. A quick note on the topic:

You can refer to the *Challenges of big data visualization* section, mentioned in `Chapter 1`, *Introduction to Big Data Visualization*, to complicate the process of identifying outliers as well.

As we've noted over and over throughout this book, the process of visualizing big data requires the aggregation or otherwise summarization of the data first (or preprocessing the data) as otherwise, effective visualization is impractical. The process of analyzing data for outliers also requires this preprocessing. In fact, the granularity (of big data) needs to be appropriately high to allow individual points to be differentiated, otherwise, outlier analysis won't be easy. To combat the difficulty of big data outlier analysis, many organizations adopt real-time outlier detection (or sometimes referred to as anomaly detection) on such data. In fact, at the time of writing, various programmable software solutions are available.

Along with this idea of the aggregation of big data into more manageable chunks is the idea of focused population definition. This is the concept of being able to reduce the big data source into much smaller views or slices of data that are focused on a particular objective (more on this concept later in this chapter).

So now as we do in each of the chapters of this book, let us explore options for addressing identified outliers in big data through the use of working examples.

Some basic examples

In the world of gaming, slot machines (a gambling machine operated by inserting coins into a slot and pulling a handle that determines the payoff) are quite popular. Most slot machines today are electronic and therefore are programmed to continuously track its activity. This provides an opportunity for our first example.

Testing slot machines for profitability

The owners of the casino want to use this data (as well as various supplementary data) to drive adjustments to their profitability strategy. In other words, what makes for a profitable slot machine? Is it the machine's theme or its type? Are newer machines more profitable (than older ones)? What about the physical location of the machine? Are lower denomination machines really profitable?

The following information is being collected:

- The **Location** of the slot machine
- **Denomination** in nickel, quarter, dollar, and so on
- **Month** of the year
- The **Weekday**
- Machine **Type** such as **4 Reel**, **5 Reel**, **Progressive**, and so on
- **Theme** of the machine (for example, **Movies**, **Entertainment**, **Horror**, and so on)
- **Age**, which is the number of months that the machine has been in service
- **Promotion** if a promotion was in progress such as **VIP**, **Monthly Player**, **Daily Special**, and so on
- **Coupons** were any coupons redeemed on this machine
- The **Weather** is the local weather on a particular day
- **Coin-in** total includes the total coins played on the machine (less payouts)

A portion of the data collected is shown in the following screenshot:

Into the outliers

Let's say you've done an appropriate amount of data reviewing. In other words, you've profiled the slot machines data and established context and quality and now let's assume that several rather simple outlier scenarios have been identified.

These include the following:

1. Penny slot machines may typically collect (based upon historic averages) one thousand dollars during an eight-hour period; however, some of the collected slot machine data recorded exceeds twice that amount (`Coin-in>1000`).

2. Mixed within the recorded **Coin-in** data there is data generated by `Video-poker` machines. The `Video-poker` machines are a type of gaming machine, but they are not categorized as a slot machine and therefore should not be included in our analysis (`Type = "Video-poker"`).

3. Slot machines are routinely replaced after 20 years of service (usually sooner) yet some of the data shows the machine age well over 20 years (`Age>20`).

4. Finally, it was observed that the **Coupons** data point only shows a single value of **None**, making this field unuseful (`Coupons = "None"`).

Having a strategy for dealing with established outlier data is important. Using that strategy, we can use Python to deal with the preceding outlier situations.

Handling excessive values

Our first outlier scenario involves information gathered from slot machines with the **Penny** denomination (**Penny** slots). These machines accept only pennies and typically have smaller payouts.

Given historical trends, **Penny** slot machines usually earn a total **Coin-in** of around 1,000 dollars over a regular period of time. During our data profiling exercise, we observed that there are penny slot machine records within our data that show **Coin-in** values over *2,000* dollars.

The following screenshot can be used to clearly illustrate the outliers identified within a portion of our slot results data:

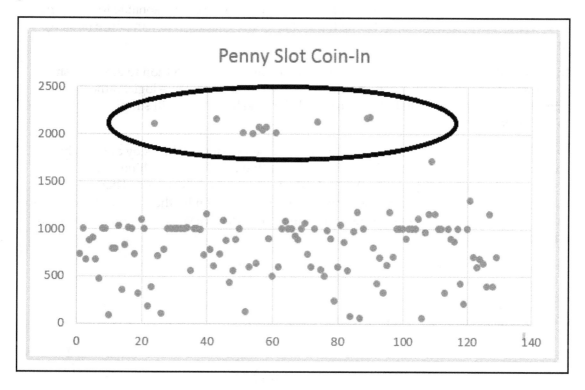

After some deliberation with the casino owners, it was decided that we should change these outlier values to the average (non-outlier) amount. In other words, we should establish an average **Coin-in** amount for penny slot machines and then identify and set all of our outlier values (those values for **Coin-in** over 2,000) to that average value.

We could assume that we already have a reasonable value to use, perhaps 1,000 (the value we previously mentioned as a penny slot average) or we could do some additional analysis on the big data source to find or calculate a more reasonable or valid average **Coin-in** value to use.

Both tasks (determine what value to use and setting outliers to a determined value) can be accomplished using Python.

Establishing the value

Practically speaking, the subject of establishing a valid or reasonable value for your outlier transformation can be pretty sophisticated (or quite simple). But it is safe to say that this analysis and related processing would be based upon some logic reasonable to a specific objective or purpose (and could be the topic of an entire chapter if not an entire book by itself).

In this chapter, we are concentrating more on the application of Python to accomplish the specific objective of establishing a particular value based upon some logic, rather than the science of what logic should be used to establish the value, so we will simply assume the following logic:

We will establish the average coin-in for all of our penny slot machines by adding the values in the field named **Coin-in** on all (and only the) penny slot machine records–excluding those (of course) with **Coin-in** values of 2,000 or more Then, we can simply do the math by dividing the accumulated total **Coin-in** by the number of penny slot machines (the number of rows of penny slot machines that we've also counted up) in our data source.

The following Python script establishes that value for us:

```
# --- simply add up the coin-in for penny slots
# --- skipping any coin-in total over 1999

import csv

with open('SlotsResults.csv') as csvfile:
    reader = csv.DictReader(csvfile)

    # --- initialize variables for the number of rows and
    # --- average coin-in amount and "x" is the running total
    # --- of coin-in

    row_count = 0
```

```
    aver_coin_in = 0.0
    x = 0.0

    for row in reader:
        if (row['Denomination']) == 'Penny':
            if int(row['Coin-in'])<2000:
                x += int(row['Coin-in'])
            row_count += 1
# --- compute the average coin-in by dividing the accumulated
# --- total of penny slit machine coin-ins by the number of penny # ---
slot machines

    aver_coin_in = x/row_count

# --- just print the calculated average coin-in

    print(aver_coin_in)
```

While we're at it, we could add variables to our script to evaluate the coin-in values (those under 2,000 for penny slot machines) and identify the MIN and MAX values. If our x variable is the sum of **Coins-in**, then y and z can be the MIN and MAX:

```
# --- AVG, MIN and MAX
import csv

with open('SlotsResults.csv') as csvfile:
    reader = csv.DictReader(csvfile)

    # --- initialize variables for the number of rows and
    # --- average coin-in amount and "x" is the running total
    # --- of coin-in, y is MIN and z is MAX

    row_count = 0
    aver_coin_in = 0.0
    x = 0.0
    y = 999
    z = 0.0

    for row in reader:
        if (row['Denomination']) == 'Penny':
            if int(row['Coin-in'])<2000:
                x += int(row['Coin-in'])
                if int(row['Coin-in'])>z:
                    z = int(row['Coin-in'])
                if int(row['Coin-in'])<y:
                    y = int(row['Coin-in'])
```

```
                    row_count += 1
# --- compute the average coin-in by dividing the accumulated
# --- total of penny slit machine coin-ins by the number of penny # ---
slot machines
      aver_coin_in = x/row_count

# --- just print the calculated average coin-in

      print("AVG:", aver_coin_in)
      print("MIN:",y)
      print("MAX:",z)
```

The following screenshot shows the result of executing our Python script within the desktop IDE Wingware (mentioned at the beginning of this chapter):

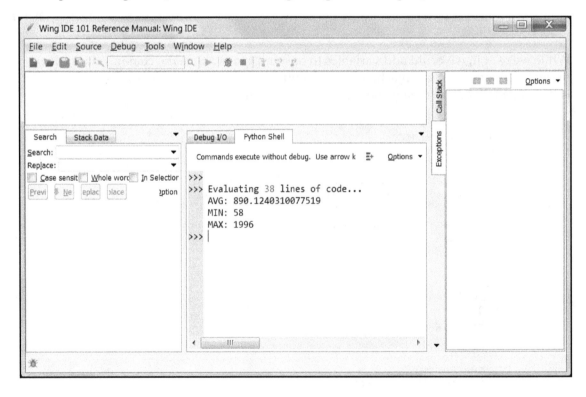

Big data note

The preceding script uses a looping approach to calculate the average coin-in value for all penny slot machines in the data. When working with big data sources you'll find that you cannot simply read through millions and millions of records expecting a result. As has been pointed out throughout this book, there is a certain amount of preprocessing of the data that needs to take place first such as narrowing your data by a time period or in this example denomination.

Setting outliers

Once we have our average coin-in value, we can then set all of the outlier values (penny slot machines with coin-in greater than 2,000) found within our data to that value (the average coin-in for all penny slot machines) using the following simple Python script:

```
# --- creating a new csv file with outlier values set to 930

import csv
with open('SlotsResults_new.csv', 'w') as csvfile_o:
    fieldnames =
['Location','Denomination','Month','Weekday','Type','Theme','Age','Promotio
n','Coupons','Weather','Coin-in']

    with open('SlotsResults_larger.csv') as csvfile:
        reader = csv.DictReader(csvfile)
        writer = csv.DictWriter(csvfile_o, fieldnames=fieldnames)

        writer.writeheader()

        for row in reader:
            if row['Coin-in']>'2000':
              x = '930'
            else:
              x = row['Coin-in']

            writer.writerow({'Location': row['Location'],
                             'Denomination': row['Denomination'],
                             'Month': row['Month'],
                             'Weekday': row['Weekday'],
                             'Type': row['Type'],
                             'Theme': row['Theme'],
                             'Age': row['Age'],
                             'Promotion': row['Promotion'],
                             'Coupons': row['Coupons'],
                             'Weather': row['Weather'],
```

```
'Coin-in': x
})
```

Removing Specific Records

Another outlier scenario encountered within our slot results gaming data is the presence of records collected from a different type of gaming machine, namely, a **Video Poker** type machine.

The following is a visualization of the gaming machine data's **Type** field:

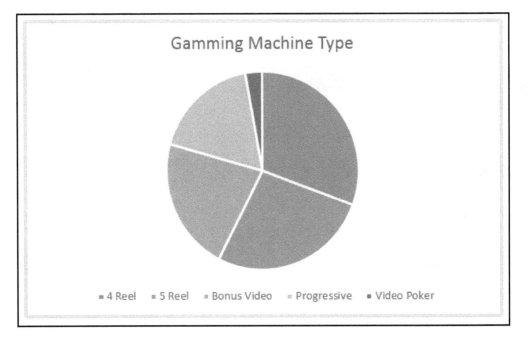

We see that data records from the video poker machines do include all of the same valid fields as the other slot machine types, such as:

- **Location**
- **Denomination**
- **Weekday**

But these records should not be included in our slot machine big data analytic project since, theoretically, the profitability of those machines may or may not be influenced by different events or other means. Also, the results from these machines may alter the perception of the results of the other types of machines.

You must have noticed **Bonus Video** type machines within our gaming data. These machines do qualify as a slot type of gaming machine and should not be confused with the **Video Poker** type.

Redundancy and risk

The data from the **Video Poker** type machines could simply be ignored in our analysis and visualization efforts, but just ignoring the data is not an effective approach.

Keeping data that is irrelevant to your objective in the project will require us to perform an explicit exclusion of that data from every logic step, path, statement, or function we perform. The question to ask yourself is, why perform the same exclusion statements over and over? More importantly, why take on the risk of forgetting to exclude the data and mistakenly including that data in your results?

Another point

Since dealing with the volumes of big data is already challenging enough, any opportunity to slim down or otherwise reduce the volume of big data you are working with should be seriously considered and will most likely be found to be advantageous.

If Type

We're quite lucky in this case, since all of these unwanted, irrelevant records are clearly and easily identifiable using the **Type** field and the conditional statement: `Type != "Video Poker"` (I'm aware that I'm using the negative here: *Not Equal To*, but as an example script; it is just easier than having to include *Equal To* in the many other machine type records found in the data).

With this in mind, the following Python script can be used to drop all of the records found in our data that are of the slot machine type **Video Poker**:

```
# --- writing a new CSV file dropping any video poker records

import csv
with open('SlotsResults.csv', 'w') as csvfile_o:
```

```
        fieldnames =
['Location','Denomination','Month','Weekday','Type','Theme','Age','Promotio
n','Coupons','Weather','Coin-in']

        with open('SlotsResults_slotonly.csv') as csvfile:

                reader = csv.DictReader(csvfile)
                writer = csv.DictWriter(csvfile_o, fieldnames=fieldnames)

                writer.writeheader()
                for row in reader:

# --- use the Type field to identify records to drop

                    if row['Type']!='Video Poker':
                        writer.writerow({'Location': row['Location'],
                                'Denomination': row['Denomination'],
                                'Month': row['Month'],
                                'Weekday': row['Weekday'],
                                'Type': row['Type'],
                                'Theme': row['Theme'],
                                'Age': row['Age'],
                                'Promotion': row['Promotion'],
                                'Coupons': row['Coupons'],
                                'Weather': row['Weather'],
                                'Coin-in': row['Coin-in']
                                })
```

Reused

You may notice that the preceding Python script appears to be practically the same as the script used in the previous section and in fact it is! We used the same logic to read our gaming file and create a new file; just altering the condition statement to test the record's **Type** field and include (write to a new **CSV** file) only those records whose **Type** field is not equal to 'Video Poker':

```
# --- if Type is not equal to a non-slot machine type then
if row['Type']!='Video Poker':
```

Changing specific values

In our third outlier scenario, we see that our slot machine data contains a field named **Age**. This field holds the value indicating the total number of years that the recording slot machine has been in service.

Since it is an established policy (in our gaming example) that slot machines have a life expectancy of only twenty years, all machines have a deliberate replacement before they reach that age (in fact, all slot machines stop incrementing years of service (its age) once the twenty years has been reached).

During the data profiling process, a number of slot machine records with an age value greater than 20 (years) were identified (as shown in the following screenshot):

These age values are considered to be outliers since they represent only an insignificant number of slot machines that are potentially beyond the standard life expectancy.

Setting the Age

In our gaming example, we want to set all slot machine records **Age** values (that are greater than 20 (years)) to 20.

The following Python script can accomplish this objective:

```
# --- creating a new csv file from our original gaming file
# --- with age set to 20 if > than 20

import csv
with open('SlotsResults_fixedAge.csv', 'w') as csvfile_o:
    fieldnames =
['Location','Denomination','Month','Weekday','Type','Theme','Age','Promotio
```

```
n','Coupons','Weather','Coin-in']

    with open('SlotsResults_larger.csv') as csvfile:
        reader = csv.DictReader(csvfile)
        writer = csv.DictWriter(csvfile_o, fieldnames=fieldnames)
        writer.writeheader()
        for row in reader:

    # --- if the age is greater than 20 make it 20
    # --- the variable x is used to reset the correct
    # --- age value

        if row['Age']>'20':
            x = '20'
        else:
            x = row['Age']

        writer.writerow({'Location': row['Location'],
                        'Denomination': row['Denomination'],
                        'Month': row['Month'],
                        'Weekday': row['Weekday'],
                        'Type': row['Type'],
                        'Theme': row['Theme'],
                        'Age': x,
                        'Promotion': row['Promotion'],
                        'Coupons': row['Coupons'],
                        'Weather': row['Weather'],
                        'Coin-in': row['Coin-in']
                        })
```

Another note

Again, we have been expeditious (perhaps maybe lazy?) in our reusing of the same Python script from earlier in this chapter! We simply changed the script that we used to modify **Coin-in** and used it to test and set the value of (slot machine) **Age**.

Keep in mind that (as I've mentioned throughout this book) there are many ways of writing Python (or any kind of) scripts and this example demonstrates just one simple approach. Simple is usually better and some trial and error (using a smaller, subset of data for your trials) are highly recommended. The readers who have been or are programmers will know that testing your logic first with a smaller subset of data is always a good practice.

Dropping fields entirely

During a typical data profiling process, each field or data point in a file is examined for its value(s). For example, as we've seen in the preceding section, the **Age** field contains a numeric value from one to twenty (along with a few outlying numbers greater than twenty, which we appropriately dealt with). We've also observed that in the **Coupons** field, there is only one value, **None**.

When a certain field contains the same value over and over, 100% of the time, it renders that field or data point useless to analysis or visualization. In other words, this condition is the same as a field being empty (containing no values at all).

The visualized values for the **Coupons** field (not very interesting at all!) is displayed in the following screenshot:

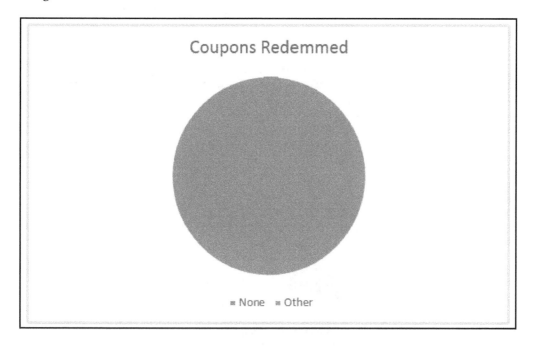

Once again, we could simply ignore the **Coupon** field when doing our analysis. In fact, it would be easier to ignore an entire field than it would be to ignore specific values within a field (as in the example discussed earlier in this section).

It is still advisable to remove the field or data point from your file, reducing the size of the file, saving (some) space and absolutely eliminating the possibility of mistakenly using the information contained within that field within a visualization.

The following Python script can be used to eliminate the specific field from the data. As before, we simply read and rewrite each record of the source file, field by field, skipping the **Coupon** field:

```python
# --- create a new file from the original file dropping the
# --- Coupons field

import csv
with open('SlotsResults_dropped_coupons.csv', 'w') as csvfile_o:
    fieldnames =
['Location','Denomination','Month','Weekday','Type','Theme','Age','Promotio
n','Weather','Coin-in']

    with open('SlotsResults_larger.csv') as csvfile:
        reader = csv.DictReader(csvfile)
        writer = csv.DictWriter(csvfile_o, fieldnames=fieldnames)
        writer.writeheader()
        for row in reader:

# --- write the fields but no Coupon field!
            writer.writerow({'Location': row['Location'],
                             'Denomination': row['Denomination'],
                             'Month': row['Month'],
                             'Weekday': row['Weekday'],
                             'Type': row['Type'],
                             'Theme': row['Theme'],
                             'Age': row['Age'],
                             'Promotion': row['Promotion'],
                             'Weather': row['Weather'],
                             'Coin-in': row['Coin-in']
                             })
```

Yes, you guessed it. Once more, we have managed to leverage pretty much the same Python script from earlier sections to drop the **Coupons** field from our data.

(This time, it's easier still as we just need to remove the references to the **Coupon** field).

More to drop

I would also advise considering dropping any additional fields (or records for that matter) that you may not initially be interested in; this will improve processing performance and save storage space.

If during your data profiling, you noticed that the data point weather is almost always recorded as hot and dry (Las Vegas, Nevada weather!), you might find that the field is not very useful, so you could go ahead and drop that field as well. In a particular analytical exercise, does the day of the week matter or is the month sufficient?

One strategy for you to consider is to generate multiple specifically focused files from the original big data source; that is, create a file that contains only the data you want to use for a certain visualization or project. More on this topic is discussed in the next section.

More examples

Effective big data statistical projects should be based on focused problem definitions. In other words, it is almost always an advantage to reduce the size of your data source (or reduce the size of the population) so that you can be more effective with the managing and manipulating of the data–yet still, produce meaningful (and correct) results.

The process of sampling or defining your population allows you the opportunity to cut down on the volume of data you need to physically process through or touch. This saves CPU cycles and more importantly, saves your time. This can also be referred to as cutting through the clutter (or noise) often so prevalent in big data sources.

Understanding that defining a population to work with on a particular big data project isn't simply truncating the records read or randomly selecting certain record subsets, is critical.

Back to a point made in an earlier section of this chapter:

An effective big data strategy may be to create files focused on a particular objective or context.

To carry this thought to another level, one can define a population focused on a particular objective. This population can be, frankly, defined in any way that makes sense to you or is appropriate to your objectives.

Because there is very rarely enough time or money to process all information available from a big data source, the goal really becomes finding a representative sample (or subset) of that population. That population can be defined as including all data with the characteristic you wish to understand.

Let's explore this concept using our sample gaming data.

A themed population

Gaming machine manufacturers often take inspiration for designing slot machines from popular culture, popular films, television shows, and other icons because players relate to these themes and are therefore more likely to want to play the machines.

Suppose our interest for a particular big data project focuses on a particular type of slot machine theme. In fact, an assumption presented to us is that horror-based slot machines continually produce below average coin-in totals unless there is a promotion offered. There is a further belief that this is only true for slot machines of a denomination less than one dollar.

As a data scientist, your first step is to create a project population definition based upon the preceding description. Given our supreme knowledge of the available gaming data (gleaned from proper data profiling sessions), we might be able to define our population using the data fields or measures namely, **Denomination**, **Theme**, and **Promotion**, as shown in the following screenshot:

Measure	Value(s)
Denomination	Dime, Nickel, Penny, Quarter, Two Cent
Theme	Horror
Promotion	None

Based upon the preceding population definition, we can create the following Python script to generate our sample population:

```
# --- let us create a sample population based upon
# --- Denomination, Theme and Promotion

import csv
with open('SlotsResults_larger_new.csv', 'w') as csvfile_o:
    fieldnames =
```

```
['Location','Denomination','Month','Weekday','Type','Theme','Age','Promotio
n','Coupons','Weather','Coin-in']

    with open('SlotsResults_larger.csv') as csvfile:

        reader = csv.DictReader(csvfile)
        writer = csv.DictWriter(csvfile_o, fieldnames=fieldnames)

        writer.writeheader()

        for row in reader:

# --- use if with or & and conditions and notice line concat

            if ((row['Denomination']=='Dime') or
(row['Denomination']=='Nickel') or \
                (row['Denomination']=='Penny') or
(row['Denomination']=='Quarter') or \
                (row['Denomination']=='Two Cent')) and
(row['Theme']=='Horror') and (row['Promotion']=='None'):
                writer.writerow({'Location': row['Location'],
                            'Denomination': row['Denomination'],
                            'Month': row['Month'],
                            'Weekday': row['Weekday'],
                            'Type': row['Type'],
                            'Theme': row['Theme'],
                            'Age': row['Age'],
                            'Promotion': row['Promotion'],
                            'Coupons': row['Coupons'],
                            'Weather': row['Weather'],
                            'Coin-in': row['Coin-in']
                            })
```

A focused philosophy

The idea of generating smaller, thinly-focused subsets (or populations) of data from much larger and widely-focused big data sources is not new or particularly innovated. Relational databases create *views* of portions or slices of data within the database that are focused and optimized for a particular use.

The idea is similar to using a pair of binoculars to zoom in on a precise area of a panoramic view of the countryside in front of you.

It's the same concept.

Summary

In this chapter, we talked about what outliers are and typical methods to deal with them. We also introduced Python as a tool to address outliers identified in your big data project.

In the next chapter, we will cover big data operational intelligence and look to address the challenges of applying basic analytics and visualization techniques to big data with Splunk.

8
Big Data Operational Intelligence with Splunk

Once there is an understanding of the challenges of applying basic analytics and visualization techniques to big data, the value of the data can be realized. This chapter offers working examples demonstrating solutions for valuing big data by gaining operational intelligence (using Splunk).

The chapter is organized into the following main sections:

- About Splunk
- Splunk and big data
- Splunk visualization – real-time log analysis
- Splunk visualization – deeper into the logs

About Splunk

Splunk originated in 2003 and was founded to pursue a disruptive new vision for making machine-generated big data easily accessible, usable, and valuable to everyone. This (machine-generated) big data can be from a wide range of sources, including websites, servers, applications, networks, mobile devices, and so on, and it can span multiple environments and even be cloud-based.

Splunk (the product), runs from both a standard command line or an interface that is totally web-based (which means that no thick client application needs to be installed to access and use the tool) and performs large-scale, high-speed indexing on both historical and real-time data.

Now you can also subscribe to the Splunk Cloud service, and get a dedicated Splunk deployment that is hosted in Amazon Web Services.

Splunk does not require a restore of any of the original data, but it stores a compressed copy of the original data (along with its indexing information) allowing you to delete or otherwise move (or remove) the original data. Splunk then utilizes this searchable repository from which to efficiently create a graph, report, alert, dashboard, and visualize in detail.

Splunk's main product is Splunk Enterprise, or simply Splunk, which was developed using C/C++ and Python for maximum performance and utilizes its own SPL for maximum functionality and efficiency.

You can literally install Splunk on any machine-virtual or physical in minutes using standard installers. It doesn't require any external packages and it drops cleanly into its own directory (usually into `c:\Program Files\Splunk`). Once installed, you can check out the `README` file, `splunk.txt` file (found in that folder) to verify the version number of the build you just installed and where to find the latest online documentation.

As the time of writing, simply going to the website `http://docs.splunk.com`will provide you with more than enough documentation to get started with any of the Splunk products and all of the information available to read online or to download in PDF format to print or read offline. In addition, it is a good idea to bookmark the Splunk Splexicon for further reference. The **Splexicon** is a cool online portal of technical terms that are specific to Splunk and all definitions include links to related information from the Splunk documentation.

Splunk and big data

Splunk has the ability to read all kinds of data-including big data–in almost any format and from any device or application.

Splunk's power is in its ability to turn data into OI or operational intelligence without the need for special parsing or adaptions to handle big data or a particular data format. Here is how it works; Splunk uses internal algorithms to learn how to process new data and new data sources automatically and efficiently. Once Splunk is aware of a new data type, you do not have to reintroduce it to Splunk in the future, saving your time.

Furthermore, since Splunk can work with both local and remote data, it is almost infinitely scalable. What this means is that your big data sources can be located on the same (physical or virtual) machine or machines as the Splunk instance you are using (meaning its local data) or on entirely different machines, practically anywhere in the world (meaning its remote data), Splunk can even take advantage of cloud-based big data!

So, let's consider some examples where we can employ Splunk with big operational data!

Splunk visualization – real-time log analysis

Enterprise applications typically continuously generate logging or messaging data in real time, allowing support personnel to monitor user activities, application events, and even the performance of processing within the application or even the application itself by reviewing this information.

The advantage of being familiar with this data may seem obvious, for example, some uses may be:

- Monitoring memory or space usage may allow administrators to be proactive and address shortages before there is an application outage
- Identifying trends in application performance can allow support personnel to resolve conflicts or errors causing degraded performance before reaching unacceptable levels

The opportunity for using application server logged information to improve performance and the level of support for an application is conceivably infinite.

Businesses are now realizing that application logging is an untapped resource in that it holds a wealth of knowledge about the business or, what is happening within the business. Using the right approach, application logging data can be used to troubleshoot a business problem or support a particular business objective.

Nevertheless, using this application-logged information, requires that an organization have a **log management strategy** (**LMS**).

An LMS will typically consist of the following:

- A collection of the logs, audit records, audit trails, event logs, and so on
- A common method for centralized log aggregation and/or indexing
- A facility for long-term log storage and retention of the logged information

- A log rotation ability (or a way of limiting the total size of the logs retained while still allowing analysis of recent events)
- Log analysis (in real time and in bulk after storage)
- Log search and reporting

In this first example, we'll use Splunk to perform some analysis, searching, and reporting of information contained in various application log files.

IBM Cognos

IBM Cognos is a popular business intelligence application and it often uses a TM1 Server as its data source. TM1 is an in-memory database that can be customized to provide forecasting, planning, and consolidation abilities (just to name a few) to small, medium, and even large global organizations. Although it is not a requirement, multiple TM1 Servers are often deployed (installed) on various machines (which may or may not be at the same location) within an organization, to serve different user communities or business objectives. All of these servers can be accessed through IBM Cognos TM1 Web, which provides multidatabase support, allowing users to access these multiple Cognos TM1 Servers (that are registered on the same Cognos TM1 Admin Server) and where users have the same username and password combination. TM1 Web can also be installed and configured on yet another machine.

All of these TM1 Servers record status messages on the activity of the server in their log files. These messages contain details on activity such as server startup and shutdown, client login events, transactional data changes, errors encountered, executed processes, chores, loaded cubes and dimensions, and synchronized replication. The extent (or level) of detail that is logged is configurable at the server level.

If one has the appropriate access, one can open, search, and view an individual server's current transaction log, from the application, but at best, this is a slow and painful process and is viewed in a typical table of transactions format.

Application log files are continually updated (as long as the server is running) and at some (predetermined) point are truncated and a new log is started. In addition, error and exception logs are generated by the server when certain events occur. All of this logging and messaging can result in a significant amount of data from each of the servers running, so attempting to perform analysis on all of the available data, generated over a span of time is nearly impossible. Unless, of course, you use Splunk.

Splunk allows you to consider all of the logs generated by all of the servers, as a single data source. It indexes all of the machine-generated data regardless of format or location allowing real-time and historical searches using the same interface!

In our example, envision the following scenario: Our organization has five groups of products that need to be forecasted, each by a different product forecasting group. Each group of users is located in a different geographical location and they use their own TM1 Server to forecast, accessed through the TM1 web interface.

Since there are currently five distinct groups of products, we are currently running five different TM1 Servers, each located on a separate **virtual machine (VM)**.

Each of the servers is running an identical product forecasting application (same features, functionalities, and purpose), but only contain data concerning a single group of product. In other words, each product group forecasts sales for only their products and on a particular TM1 Server. At certain intervals, we'll assume all forecast data for all products is replicated to a reporting application where it is consolidated and reviewed. Product groups are measured and rewarded on not only the accuracy of their forecasts, but also on the time it takes to enter, review, adjust, approve, and report their forecast efforts. Over time, various groups have complained that their server isn't up and available as much as they would like and the time it takes for system maintenance (such as data loading) to be performed is increasing.

The following is our **TM1 Server** architecture:

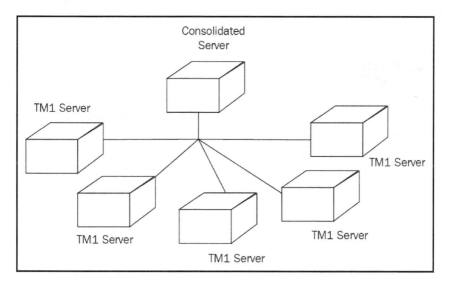

As we've mentioned earlier, each individual TM1 Server is continually generating logging information. To effectively monitor our TM1 Servers, we want to visualize all of the server logs as a single big data operational data source.

So, let's get started!

To start monitoring with Splunk (or actually to do pretty much anything with Splunk), you need to feed it some type of data. Once Splunk becomes aware of your data, it instantly indexes it so that it's available for searching and analyzing purposes. At that point, the data has been transformed into Splunk events (each with its own set of searchable fields).

Splunk is particularly efficient in dealing with all IT streaming, machine, and historical data.

MS Windows event logs, web server logs, live application logs, network feeds, system metrics, change monitoring, message queues, archive files, or anything else of interest–including our Cognos TM1 Server logs–can be easily monitored using Splunk.

The following are the steps to begin monitoring big data with Splunk:

- Point Splunk at your big data or a source of big data
- Provide some details about the big data/data source (that then becomes a Splunk data input)

Splunk then begins to index the big data/data source (transforming it into searchable events) allowing you to begin searching and monitoring your big data.

Pointing Splunk

Once you have logged into your Splunk instance, you can click on the menu (in the upper right of the page) titled **Settings**, and then click on the **Add Data** image (as shown in the following screenshot):

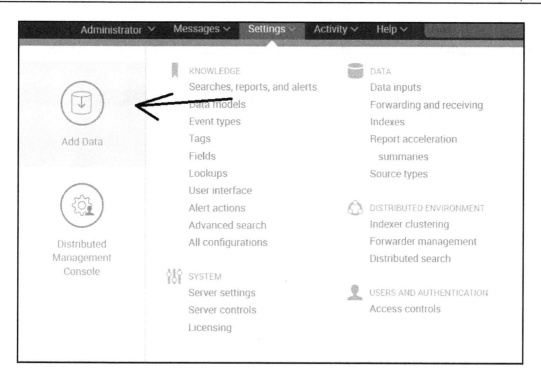

From there, select **monitor** (found in the middle of the page and shown in the following screenshot):

Once on the Splunk **Add Data** page (shown in the following screenshot), use the scroll bar to move through the list displayed on the left of the page and locate and select **Files & Directories**:

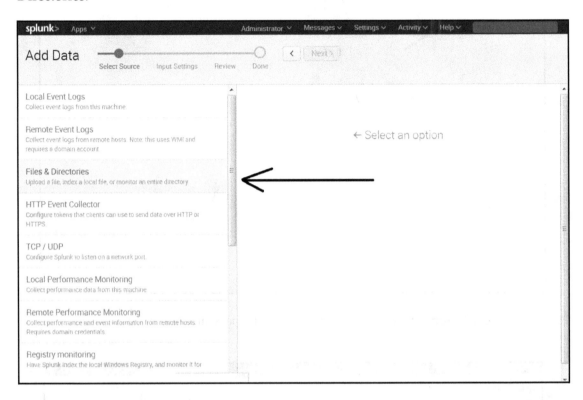

Since we want to continuously monitor all of the log files that each TM1 Server generates (not just a single log file), we'll point Splunk to the folders where the servers write and update files (rather than selecting an individual file). Splunk makes accomplishing this easy by letting you browse or navigate to the desired (logging) folder.

Once you've selected the folder, you can add **Whitelist** and**Blacklist** parameters, if you wish to. These parameters can be used to apply regular expressions to tell Splunk to explicitly include or exclude certain file(s) found in the designated folder (again in our example, we'll allow Splunk to include all the files in the logging folders).

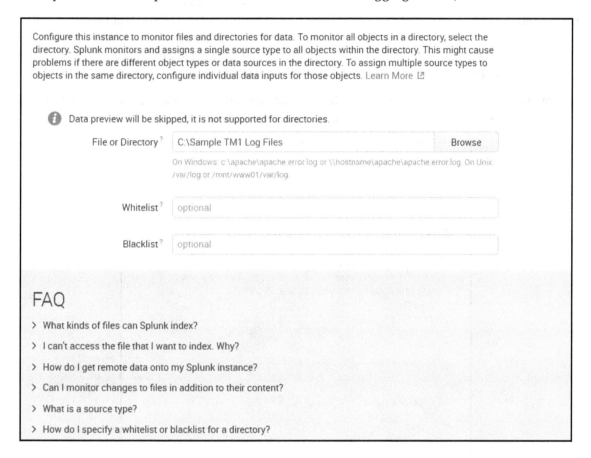

After you've selected the desired (logging) folder, click on the button at the top of the page labeled **Next** (shown in the following screenshot):

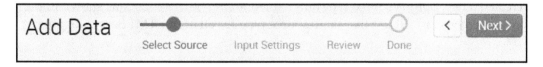

On Splunk's **Input Settings** page, you can specify a **Source type**, **App context**, and **Host**. **App context** and **Host** are important parameters, but for our example, the most important parameter is the **Source type**.

The **Source type** parameter is one of the defaults that Splunk assigns to all incoming data. It tells Splunk what kind of data you've got, so that Splunk can format the data intelligently during indexing. Since we have multiple folders containing the application log files we wish to monitor, we can designate a source type for the log files so that all incoming TM1 logs will be organized and indexed quickly and similarly.

By default, Splunk sets the source type to **Automatic** (so that it can just deal with it), but you can select from known **Source Type** or create a new type.

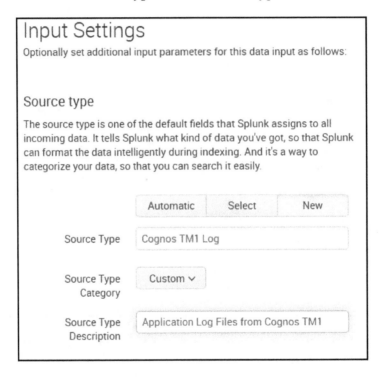

I've created a new Splunk source type and named it `Source TM1 Log` (as shown in the preceding screenshot). I'll use this same source type for all of our TM1 Server logging folders.

Once you add a new source type, it's easy to select again when we add the next logging folder (as shown in the following screenshot).

If you forget to set the source type when adding a folder, you can go back and change the source type later.

When you have completed reviewing and selecting the Input settings, you can click on the button labeled **Review** (shown in the following screenshot):

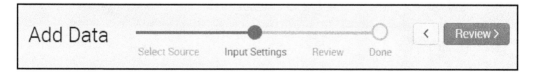

Splunk then displays the following screenshot with the details of the input source you just set up for you to review:

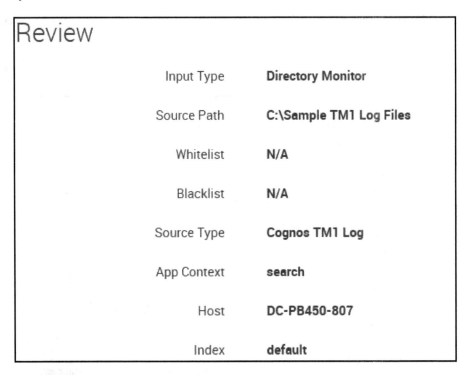

Lastly, you click on the button labeled **Submit** (shown in the following screenshot):

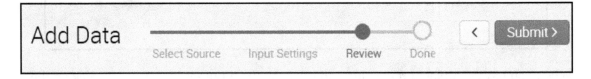

As the following page indicates, we are now ready to begin using Splunk to visualize our application log big data contained in the c:\Sample TM1 Log Files folder.

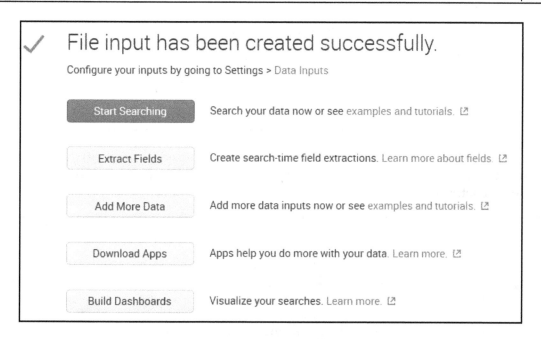

Once you have pointed Splunk to all (five) of your TM1 server logging folders and set each folder to the same (that is, the `Cognos TM1 Log` file) **Source type** (shown in the following screenshot), you can then perform searches using that single source type and Splunk will consider all of the data in all of the folders as a single input source.

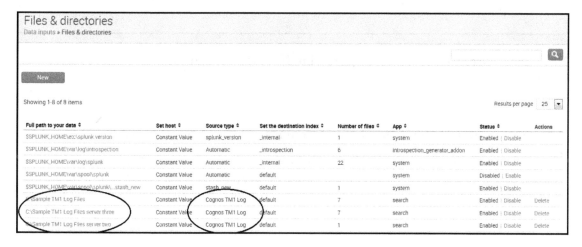

Let's try this out with some simple Splunk searches.

From the Splunk Search page, we could simply type:

```
sourcetype="Cognos TM1 Log"
```

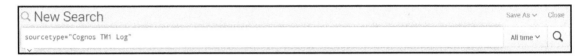

This will search all of the data that Splunk currently has indexed (is aware of) that has the same source type (the `Cognos TM1 Log` file) and list the transactions or events it finds (there are a lot!):

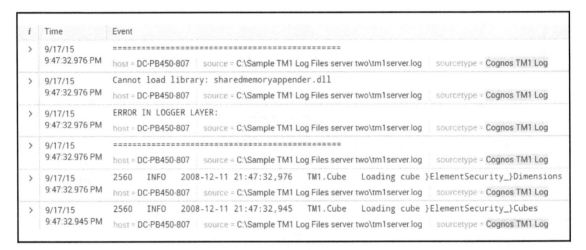

Now, let us narrow down that searching a bit. If we modify our original search to the following:

```
sourcetype="Cognos TM1 Log" date_month=february
```

We will tell Splunk to only return events found that occurred in February.

 Splunk provides the ability for you to define custom fields within your data, but it also is intelligent enough to give you a list of fields it finds on its own. The `date_month` is an example of a field that Splunk found.

With an interest in application support (of our TM1 Servers), we might ask the question, "How many times were TM1 Servers shut down during the month of February?" Having worked with TM1 in the past, we know that TM1 Servers log all events (including when the server is shut down) by writing a record in the log file such as the following:

[]INFO 2015-02-05 16:55:53.593 TM1.ServerServer shutdown

So now we can alter our Splunk search again to include a reference to the phrase shutdown (the asterisk is used as a wildcard character to match an unlimited number of characters in a string):

```
sourcetype="Cognos TM1 Log" date_month=february shutdown*
```

Now, Splunk returns 26 matches or **Events** found within our data source:

So, we can now understand from our data that given our five TM1 Servers, 26 shutdown events have occurred during the month of February.

Can we now visualize that information with Splunk?–thankfully, it's pretty easy:

From the search page, click on the tab labeled **Visualization**:

Next, select **Pivot**:

Splunk will ask us if we want to consider using all of the fields in the data in our visualization; for now, let's just say yes by selecting the option button labeled **All Fields (17)**:

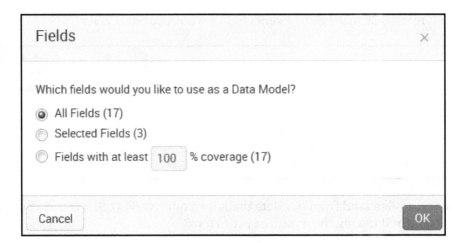

Once you've clicked on **OK** on the **Fields** dialog (as shown in the following screenshot), from the Splunk **New Pivot** page, we can set the **Split Rows**, **Split Columns**, and **Column Values** to be used by Splunk to create a pivot table that our visualization will be based upon:

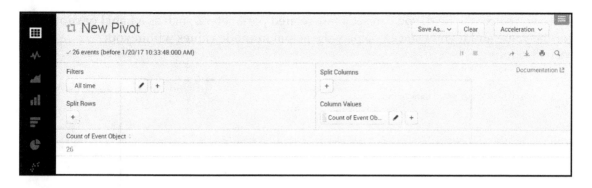

Setting rows and columns

To choose which data fields to use as the pivot's rows and columns, you can click on the +
buttons. Splunk then provides a list of fields to choose from. For the rows, we can select the
field date_month field:

Once you select the field, you can set a few related parameters, such as a **Label** or caption for the value and if you want to display the actual numeric values within your visualization:

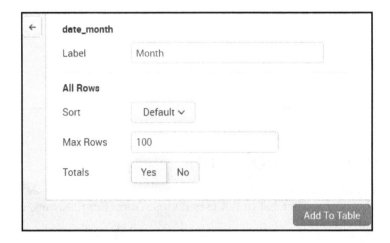

For the columns, we can again click on the + button and select `date_mday`:

Finally, using the toolbar located on the left side of the**New Pivot** page (shown in the following screenshot), we can select a visualization type for Splunk to create for us (I've chosen an **Area Chart**):

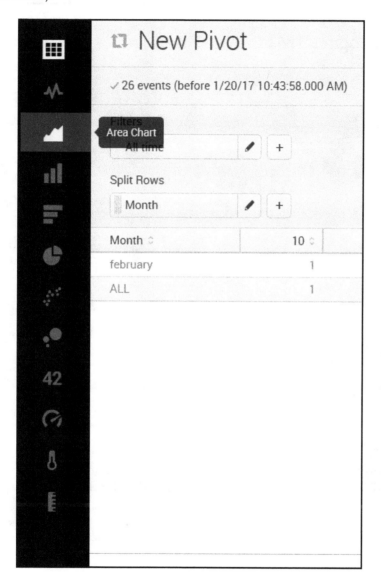

And so Slunk builds us our first big data visualization showing the count of server shutdown events that occurred in the month of February, split by the day of the month:

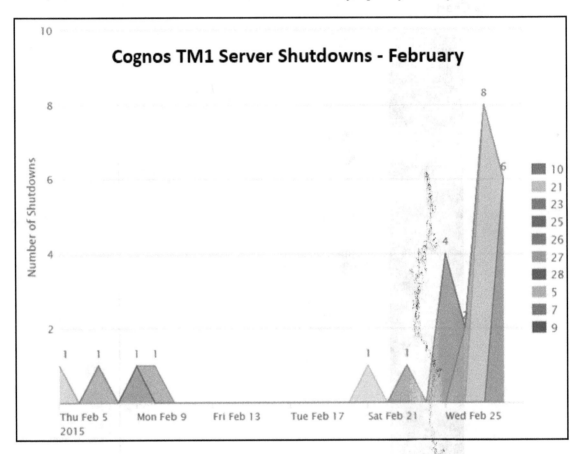

 There are various ways to enhance this visualization, for example, re-ordering the display of the days of the week, adding a baseline, changing colors, adding titles, and so on. The reader should take a time to explore and experiment!

Possibly another view of this information would be interesting to the support staff. Back on the**New Pivot** page, let's change the **Split Columns** to date_wday:

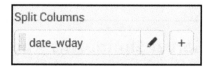

Next, let us select pie chart as our visualization type and then review and set certain parameters (shown in the following screenshot) such as the **Field** to drive **Color** in the visualization, add some labels or captions, and so on.

This effort gives us the following visualization, which indicates the breakdown of server shutdown events by the days of the week, including a nice mouse-over popup that provided the details behind each day:

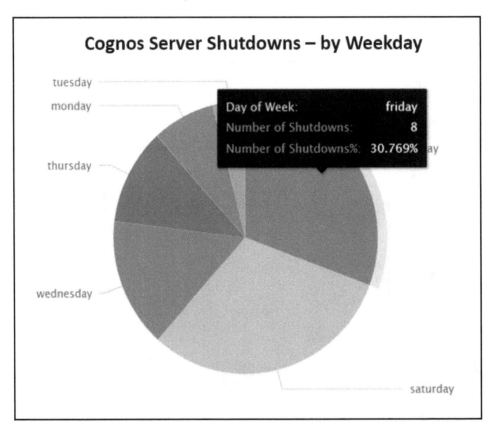

It should be noted that all of the Splunk visualizations you create on your big data input source can easily be saved and used as a dynamic report or as a panel within a Splunk dashboard (more on this later in this chapter).

Finishing with errors

In Cognos TM1, an application administrator can create **TurboIntegrator**
(**TI**) processes and save the processes on an IBM Cognos TM1 Server. The administrator
also assigns security privileges to the TurboIntegrator processes and users must have access
privileges to execute the TurboIntegrator processes. A TurboIntegrator process contains a
script of functions and commands to programmatically import data as well as create and
modify TM1 objects, such as cubes and dimensions. Even with extensive testing efforts,
sometimes these processes finish executing with errors. Those who support the TM1 Servers
need to have information about these errors. Since we have five TM1 Servers running
continuously in five distinct and separate locations, all constantly creating logging and
messaging information, it is somewhat difficult to monitor all of these logs for processing
errors.

Splunk and processing errors

Once again, Splunk offers an easy way to monitor all of the server logs for individual events
in this case TurboIntegrator processing errors. Let's look at an example.

From the Splunk search page, we can use the following:

```
source=* "finished executing with errors"
```

From the results, we should take note of the **Selected Fields** (displayed on the left of the
page):

Specifically, note the **source** field value of four. If we click on the field, we can see the details of the **source** field (shown in the following screenshot):

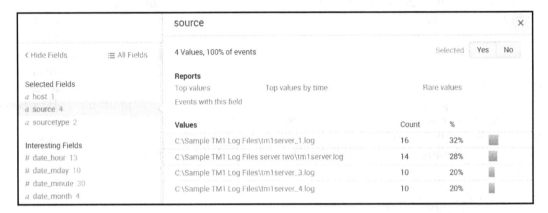

One can see that processing errors have occurred in four of the TM1 Servers (based upon finding the phrase `"finished executing with errors"` in all of the four logging folders listed).

Now, let's put together a quick, simple visualization based upon the information that Splunk has derived from our big data source.

As we did earlier in this section, we can click on the tab labeled **Visualization**, and then click on the image **Pivot**. From there, once again we will keep **Fields** default **All Fields (17)**.

Now, we should be back at the **New Pivot** page, where we can set the values we want Splunk to use in our visualization. We'll use the source as the **Split Rows** value (I've named it TM1 Server) and linecount as the **Split Columns** value:

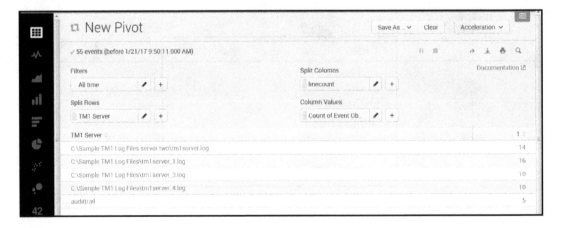

Finally, I selected bar chart for the visualization type this time (shown in the following screenshot):

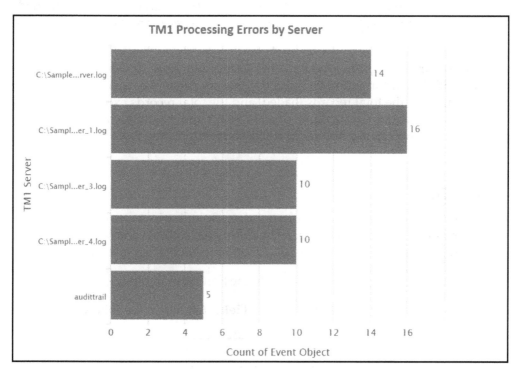

One might see how a dynamic report or dashboard of this time would be valuable information to an application support person.

Let's look at one more example of using Splunk to monitor events generated by multiple online application servers.

Splunk visualization – deeper into the logs

We spoke about TurboIntegrator earlier in this chapter. TurboIntegrator is the Cognos TM1 ETL scripting language used to (among other things) load data from external data sources into a TM1 server. These TI scripts can read directly from most data sources and can also easily load data from text or **CSV** files. Most organizations create multiple TI scripts, test and then schedule them to execute on a routine schedule, to keep the information within TM1 up to date.

In a mature organization (or one that follows proven-practice methodologies), ETL scripts should generate load or processing statistics. These stats can then be used for many things such as determining the success of the executed process (records read = records loaded), performance trending (using the duration time of the processes, are they beginning to run slower over time?), and so on.

In our example, our organizations load process scripts and write statistics upon conclusion or successful end. This information includes the process name, the run date, the duration, the total records read, the total records loaded, and the total records excepted (not loaded), and so on. This information is saved in a process folder and eventually archived to a separate area where we can use Splunk to create some interesting visualizations.

New fields

In Splunk, once you've set up a source for your data, Splunk tries to determine (or extract) as many fields as it can so that you can use them for your analysis and visualizations. Of course, you always have the opportunity to extract new fields from your data.

To extract additional fields, you can navigate to the Splunk search page, and then:

1. Click on the link labeled **Extract New Fields** (shown in the following screenshot):

2. From there, Splunk steps you through the process of creating new fields on the **Extract Fields** page (shown in the following screenshot). The first step is to select a Splunk source or **Source type** and then click on the button labeled **Next**:

3. From there, you can use a regular expression to parse or extract data as a new field or use a delimiter. For our example, we can click on the image marked **Delimiters**, as shown in the following screenshot:

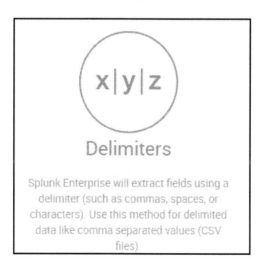

4. Next, select the delimiter you wish to use (**Space**, **Comma**, **Tab**, **Pipe**, or **Other**). In our example file, the delimiter is the comma. Once I select the**Comma**, Splunk immediately parses our data into the five fields we expect identified as **field1** through **field5** (shown in the following screenshot):

5. If you click on the edit icon to the right of each field, Splunk gives you the opportunity to provide a more meaningful name:

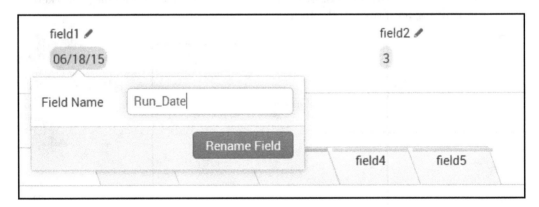

6. After I rename the fields (type the new field name and then click on **Rename Field**), we now have `Run_date`, `Duration`, `Records_Read`, `Records_Loaded`, and `Exceptions`:

7. After we have renamed all of our fields, we click on **Next** and Splunk asks us to provide an **Extractions Name** and set **Permissions** as to which users can access them:

Done! Now we are ready to use our new fields to create a new big data visualization.

For example, we could construct a simple search statement using the `Run_Date` field to search for all of the data load events that occurred in January 2016:

```
sourcetype=LoadTimes Run_Date=01/*/16
```

The `sourcetype=LoadTimes` restricts our search to our single input source and then we reference the newly extracted `Run_Date` field to narrow the search to show only the ones we are interested in:

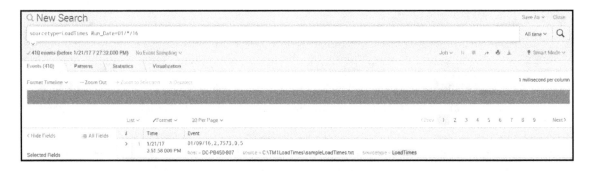

As we did earlier in this chapter, we can again click on the tab labeled **Visualization**, click on **Pivot**, and then select **All Fields**. On the **New Pivot** page, we can select `Run_Date` for the **Split Rows** and `Run_Date` (again) as the **Split Columns**. Be sure to set **Sum of Duration** as the **Column Values**:

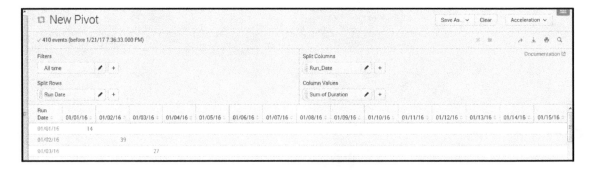

Lastly, we can select column chart for the visualization type. With some experimentation with labels and captions, we get a pretty respectable visualization showing the duration (in minutes) of the daily data load process for each day in January 2016:

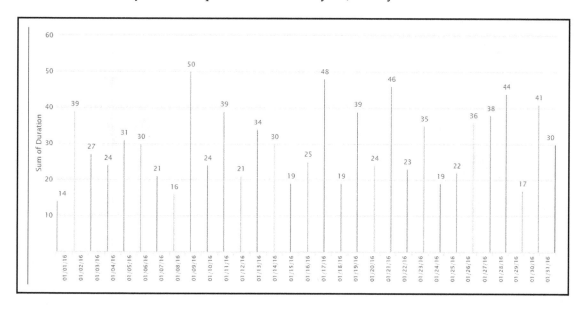

Let's take this one step farther and save the visualization as a Splunk dashboard.

To do that, you can simply click on the menu labeled **Save As...** and then select **Dashboard Panel**.

The new **Dashboard Panel** dialog box then allows you to assign a name for your new dashboard and panel as well as set the proper access allowing others to share your new dashboard:

Splunk notifies you once your dashboard is created (shown in the following screenshot) and to view your dashboard, you can click on **View Dashboard**:

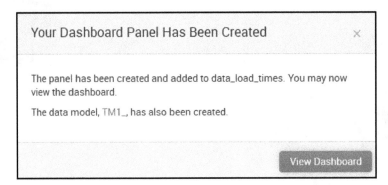

Viola! We have a Splunk big data dashboard!

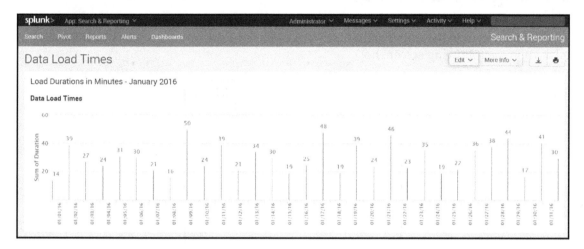

Perhaps, though we might want to compare run times from January of the prior year in the same dashboard, there are several ways to accomplish this, but the general idea is that you:

1. Recreate the search (similar to the January 2016 search we just completed).
2. Use the new search results to create a visualization (just like we did for the 2016 search).
3. Save the new visualization as a dashboard panel (again, just like we did for the 2016 column chart, as shown in the preceding screenshot).

Editing the dashboard

Once you have your new dashboard panel saved, you can reopen our dashboard and click on the menu item in the upper right of the page labeled **Edit**, and then select **Edit Panels** (shown in the following screenshot):

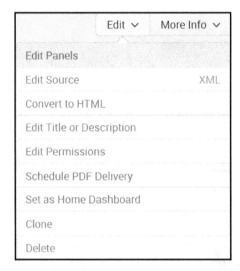

Next, click on the button labeled + Add Panel (shown in the following screenshot):

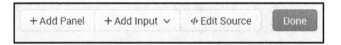

The **Add Panel** dialog appears:

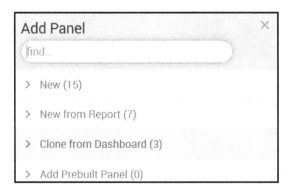

On the **Add Panel** dialog, you could select **New** if you wanted to create the new panel from here (or you could use an existing report or prebuilt panel–these are the options the reader should review), but we have already created our panel, so we click on **Clone from Dashboard**, which then lists dashboard panels available to select and include.

The panel named **2015 Data Load Times** is the panel that I have already created as described earlier. **Data Load Times** was the initial panel we created and is already part of our dashboard:

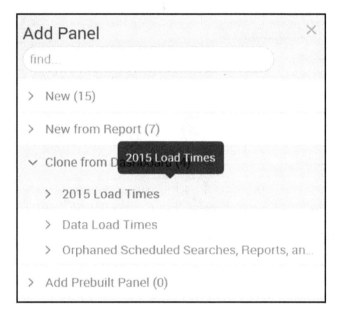

When I click on the **2015 Load Times** panel, Splunk provides a preview of the panel:

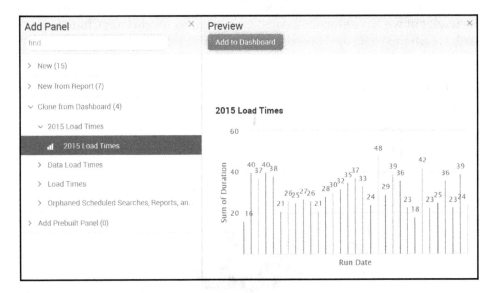

Yes, that's the one I want, so I can click on the button at the top of the preview dialog labeled **Add to Dashboard**. The following is our two paneled Splunk big data dashboard:

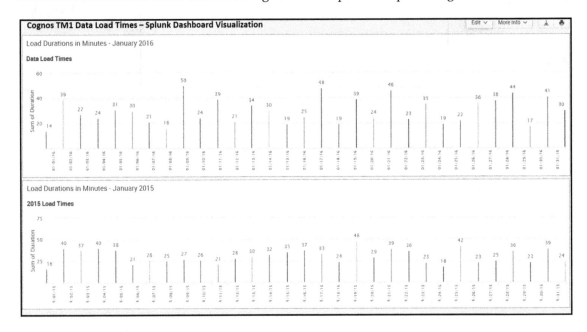

More about dashboards

In Splunk, dashboards are described as a type of view, and that view is made up of panels like the two simple ones we just created. Panels can contain objects known as modules such as **Search boxes**, **Fields**, **Charts**, **Tables**, and **Lists**. You can make your dashboard simple and straightforward (like our data load example) or very complex and sophisticated. To help with the more complex efforts, Splunk provides a dashboard editor that gives you a starting framework for your dashboard and then gives you the tools to customize your dashboard in numerous ways.

Summary

In this chapter, we started with a short discussion on what Splunk is and how it can potentially be used to harness the value of big data; specifically, with the machine or application-generated operational big data. We also considered several working examples using Splunk to search and then visualize the application server log files.

It should be noted that the examples provided in this chapter were, however, realistic, but also somewhat modest and that Splunk is a mature, robust tool that offers functions and features much too numerous for the scope of this book.

As an aside, I recommend joining the online Splunk community (it's excellent!) or checking out the many wonderful and helpful Splunk books available today, including mine, *Mastering Splunk, Packt Publishing, 2014.*

Index

Splunk, used for monitoring 269, 270, 271
Splunk, visualization 249, 250, 271, 272
reliability 134, 135, 136
rows
setting 263, 264, 265, 266, 267, 268

S

sales transactions example
about 181, 182
context, adding 182
data, visualizing 196
data, wrangling 183, 184, 188, 189, 190, 192, 193, 194, 195
Tableau dashboard 197, 198, 200, 201, 202, 203, 204, 205
work, presenting 207, 208
workbook, saving 206
Scalable Vector Graphics (SVG) 144
Search Processing Language (SPL) 35
slot machines
Age values, setting 239
big data 235
big data, volume reducing 237
excessive values, handling 231, 232
fields, dropping 241, 242
onto outliers 230
outliers, setting 235
processing performance, improving 243
Python script, writing 240
redundancy 237
risk 237
specific record, removing 236, 237
specific values, modifying 238, 239
testing, for profitability 229, 230
value, establishing 232
Software as a Service (SaaS) 47
Splexicon 248
Splunk
about 247, 248
reference 248
visualization, with real-time log analysis 249, 250, 271, 272
working, with big data 248, 249
Stacked Area
viewing, via Nest template 173, 174, 175, 176,
177
Stacked-to-Multiples
URL 156
Structured Query Language (SQL) 180

T

Tableau Desktop 180
Tableau Public 180
Tableau Reader 180
Tableau Server 180
Tableau
about 179
and big data 180, 181
filtering feature 210
products 180
reference 180
tools 209, 210, 211
TM1 Server
architecture 251
transitioning 160
Trifacta
about 181
reference 181
TurboIntegrator (TI) 269

V

variety 15
velocity 14
virtual machine (VM) 251
Visual Basic Script (VBScript) 111
Visual Query Language (VizQL) 180
visualization
philosophies 21
real-time log analysis, with Splunk 249, 250, 271, 272
strategies 23, 24
variety 22
velocity 22
volume 22, 23
volume
about 14
reference 14

W
Wingware